YOU Got THIS!

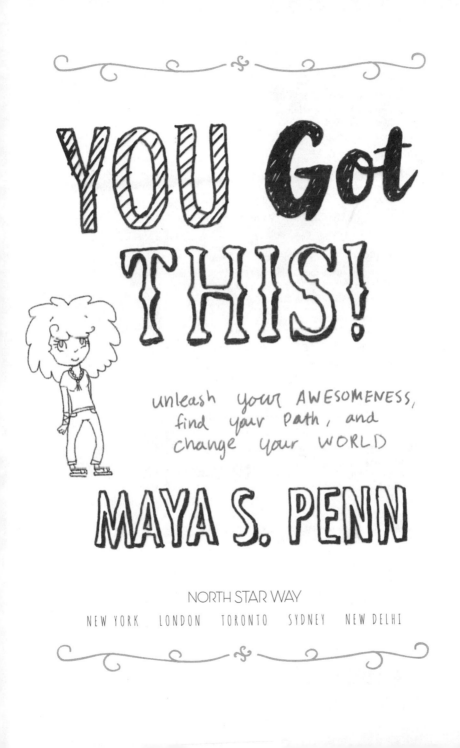

unleash your AWESOMENESS,
find your path, and
change your WORLD

MAYA S. PENN

NORTH STAR WAY

NEW YORK   LONDON   TORONTO   SYDNEY   NEW DELHI

North Star Way
An Imprint of Simon & Schuster, Inc.
1230 Avenue of the Americas
New York, NY 10020

First North Star Way hardcover edition April 2016

NORTH STAR WAY and colophon are trademarks of Simon & Schuster, Inc.

All line art courtesy of Maya S. Penn

For information about special discounts for bulk purchases, please
contact Simon & Schuster Special Sales at 1-866-506-1949 or
business@simonandschuster.com.

The North Star Way Speakers Bureau can bring authors to your live event. For
more information or to book an event contact the North Star Way Speakers
Bureau at 1-212-698-8888 or visit our website at www.thenorthstarway.com.

Interior design by Jaime Putorti

Manufactured in the United States of America

10 9 8 7 6 5 4 3 2 1

Library of Congress Cataloging-in-Publication Data
Names: Penn, Maya, author.
Title: You got this! : unleash your awesomeness, find your path, and change
    your world / Maya Penn.
Description: First North Star Way hardcover edition. | New York : North
    Star Way, [2016]
Identifiers: LCCN 2015037980| ISBN 9781501123719 (hardcover) | ISBN
    9781501117664 (ebook)
Subjects: LCSH: Vocational guidance--Juvenile literature. |
    Self-realization--Juvenile literature. | Social action--Juvenile
    literature. | BISAC: JUVENILE NONFICTION / General. | SELF-HELP /
    Creativity. | BODY, MIND & SPIRIT / Inspiration & Personal Growth.
Classification: LCC HF5381.2 .P4195 2016 | DDC 650.1--dc23
LC record available at http://lccn.loc.gov/2015037980

ISBN 978-1-5011-2371-9 (HC)
ISBN 978-1-5011-1766-4 (ebook)

Dedicated to my grandmother
Marguerite Flanders

CONTENTS

Contents

INTRODUCTION

I was standing in the dark, waiting in the wings of the auditorium, and I could barely hear the boom of the speakers over the *thump thump thump* of my heart in my chest. A few chuckles rang out from the audience—being projected onto a massive screen at the center of the stage was a digital animation short I had worked on for months. (It had taken *days* to get the characters' mouths to move in time to the voice-over on the audio track, weeks to get the story, the dialogue, and the graphics just right.) I took a few short, shallow breaths. I tried to steady my nerves. I resisted the urge to crush the plastic water bottle I had been turning over and over in my hands. And just when I thought I might vibrate right out of my socks, I heard my mother's voice ringing in my ears. "Maya," she had said calmly, when I admitted to her just how nervous I really was, "*do it afraid.*"

When the projection ended and the house lights went up, I took a few wobbly (albeit determined) steps forward. I was only vaguely aware of the applause, the friendly whoops and cheers from the crowd. I found my way to my mark—that iconic circle of red carpet, right in the center of the stage—and looked out into a sea of faces. Hundreds and hundreds of faces. All of them waiting to hear what *I* had to say.

I felt my stomach flip-flop and my heart flutter.

I was thirteen years old. I'd flown 2,500 miles from my hometown of Atlanta, Georgia, to San Francisco to do this. I had been practicing my speech for longer than I cared to admit. But there was only one thought echoing in my head:

I can't believe I'm actually here.

Just five years earlier, I'd been a quirky, awkward eight-year-old kid. (I'm not eight anymore, obviously, but the "quirky, awkward" part hasn't changed much.) I was a decent tennis player and a pretty good pianist. I loved drawing and doodling and watching cartoons. In fact, I was almost always doing something creative. That creative drive soon led me to try my hand at clothing design: I began making headbands from scraps of discarded fabric I found around the house. When I started wearing those headbands out in public—and getting lots of compliments on my designs—it occurred to me that I might be able to sell those creations. With no business plan and no experience running, well, *anything*, I became a professional fashion designer and Maya's Ideas, my eco-friendly clothing company, was born. Fast-forward a few months, and *Forbes* magazine came calling (they wanted to run a feature on the pint-sized CEO and "kid entrepreneur"), which started a snowball of sorts: I was profiled in a bunch of other magazines, and even made television appearances (the *Steve Harvey* show and *The View*, to name just a few). My company exploded. Before long, I'd earned enough to begin donating between 10 and 20 percent of my profits to charities and environmental organizations, as well as to fund my future college education. I launched my second venture, Maya's Ideas 4 The Planet, a 501(c)(3) nonprofit. I met some amazing and world-renowned people, received a slew of honors and awards, and became a national spokesperson and a brand ambassador. I was even invited to sit on a grant-making advisory board. Still, nothing could have prepared me for the annual TEDWomen event, where I was supposed to give a speech to an audience of, potentially, millions.

After all, I was (and still am) just a kid!

So there I was, standing on the red circle of carpet in the center of the TEDWomen stage, quaking and shaking in my Toms shoes. If you're not familiar, TED events (short for technology, entertainment, and design) are global conferences; the whole point is for a bunch of people to come together to, in the words of the conference organizers, "share ideas and spark conversation." My role, specifically as one of eight speakers appearing on the first day of the three-day event, was to tell my story in the hope of inspiring other women and girls to be "creators and change makers." I had hoped that, while giving my talk, I'd come off cool as a cucumber. Internally, however, I felt a huge lack of coolness. (Potatoes, maybe. Or some other vegetable far less cool and . . . cucumbery.) I wanted to be present and focused, but standing up there was a bit like having an out-of-body experience. My lips were moving, but I had no idea what I was actually saying. (I mean, I *did*, but I also didn't. It's pretty tough to explain.)

Ryan Lash / TED

At the halfway point of my speech, though, something interesting happened. I had stopped to show the audience another one of my animations, and for the first time all afternoon, I was kind of able to catch my breath. I realized that the stage, which I had thought would be *colossal*, that I'd feel as tiny as a grain of sand on a beach, was actually not all that big. It was relatively snug, in fact. Almost comfortable. (Actually, don't tell the TED staff, but I had an urge to just lie down and curl up on that bright red circle of carpet, I was suddenly enjoying myself so much.) I think I'd always known, despite my nerves, that if I just gave it my best shot, this whole speaking-to-an-audience-of-strangers thing would turn out okay. I was pleased that I was starting to get the hang of it. But then, as I was concluding my speech and delivering my last line—about the importance of understanding the challenges facing our world not with your *head*, but with your heart—I saw that the crowd wasn't just clapping and cheering . . .

I was getting a standing ovation!

You know how sometimes it takes a while for things to sink in? Something truly wonderful might happen to you, but you're so shocked and stunned that you can't appreciate it right away? Let me tell you, this was nothing like that. The rush of pride I felt was immediate. All I'd wanted was to get through my speech without falling right off the stage or flubbing my lines, and what I got was so much better than that. I practically floated down to my seat in the audience and sat there with a big silly grin on my face.

That TEDWomen talk—the one I'd almost been too nervous to give—has since gone viral, racking up more than 1.2 million views. If you can believe it (and most of the time, *I* can't), it's actually ranked among the most-viewed TEDWomen talks of all time. Since stepping off the stage, I've turned into something of a role model. I'm fifteen now as I write this, but I'm often asked to give advice, even to folks who are much, much older than me. And while some of those people are genuinely interested in my story—they want to know how an eight-year-old managed to launch her own business—most of the people I hear from are far more curious about how they might go about pulling off something unexpected, or bold, or inspiring, too:

"How can I turn my dreams into an actual, practical reality?"

"How can I get paid to do what I love?"

"How can I get people to listen to me? To respect me? To support my ideas?"

"How can I possibly make a difference, especially if I'm still just a kid?"

Those questions—and many more like them—are what this book is about: how to discover your passion, how to turn that passion into action, and how to find your place in the world.

Before we get off on the wrong foot here, let me be honest: I still have plenty of questions myself. I used to think that to *be* a really accomplished person, you had to *act* like a really accomplished person. I act like a goofy, awkward little jelly bean. Sometimes I wonder what people must imagine when they think about my life: that I spend all my time sitting at my computer, crunching numbers, drowning in a sea of packing tape and shipping receipts. That's definitely not me, either. (More often than not, I'm probably sitting around thinking about Pokémon cheats.) I have, however, learned some tips and tricks that just might help you on your journey, and what I can tell you for certain is this: you have no idea how big an idea can get when you have the courage to follow your heart. One day you're sitting around making headbands, the next you're doing a TED talk in front of millions of people. It's weird, but that kind of crazy, unimaginable stuff happens every day. All it takes is one person, one vision, one voice.

So, how do you get there? How do you get started? How do you effect real and meaningful change? You start by getting out of your own way, putting aside your doubts, and having faith that if you give it your best shot, things really will turn out okay. You start by taking that first step onto the stage. Sometimes you start by doing it afraid. Picking up this book is a good way to get started, too.

I've organized this book so that it's like a journey of sorts. In part I, we'll talk a little about the power of creativity and the joy of pursuing your passions. (What are *you* passionate about? Do you want to start a business of your own? Make a change in your community? Found a club at your school?) In part II, we'll tackle how to start putting those passions—whatever they are—into action. And in part III, we'll talk about how one person, even a very young person, has the power to change the world. (Still not convinced? I'll share some stories of other kids who are unleashing their awesomeness and changing their worlds, too.)

So don't worry if you don't yet have a clue about what you want to do in this life: I'll give you tips to help you discover it. Don't worry if "changing the world" sounds beyond the scope of your wildest dreams; together, we'll take it one step at a time. Don't worry if you feel small, or insignificant, or like your voice isn't big enough or special enough to be heard. We all feel like that sometimes—even me.

Here's the thing, though: if I can do it, there's certainly no reason why you can't do it, too. I believe that everyone has been blessed with a purpose, a passion, and the tools to pursue that passion. What you need to succeed is already in you. All you have to do is turn the page.

Believe me when I tell you: you got this!

· PART ONE ·

Unleash Your Awesomeness

I've always thought of myself as an artist. In fact, I've been drawing and doodling and scribbling since I was old enough to hold a crayon. I'm not sure if my parents gave me so many art supplies because I'd expressed an interest in drawing or because they just wanted to give me something to *do*, but I always had a fair amount of markers and colored pencils to work with; we still have boxes and boxes of all the "art" I made as a little kid. And I still vividly remember lying on the floor of the living room, sketching intently in my notebook (and by "notebook" I mean a stack of bright-colored construction paper).

Like all kids, I mostly drew the usual stuff: my parents, my extended family, and me (in stick-figure form, of course), cats and dogs, trees and flowers, and the occasional forest animal. Sometimes I'd sketch popular Nickelodeon or Disney characters, like Mickey Mouse,

SpongeBob SquarePants, or Donald Duck. Sometimes I'd invent my own characters. For example, I had a whole series of drawings about three dogs—the Barking Brothers—all of whom were named after berries. (Blueberry, Blackberry, and Raspberry, if you're wondering. And, yes, they were all drawn in a color that matched their namesake fruit.) The Barking Brothers went on lots of adventures, although the only one I really remember involved a pirate ship for some reason. I'm not sure if they hijacked the ship, or maybe they just owned one. (Perhaps they were pirate dogs?) I just know they went on some kind of journey across the open ocean. Hey, don't judge me. I was only three, maybe four years old.

Anyway, it's probably not a big surprise that in addition to being a lover of drawing, I have also always been a major fan of cartoons. When I was little, I mostly watched Playhouse Disney—*The Wiggles*, *Rolie Polie Olie*, and all those shows—in the mornings before getting my schoolwork started. When I got a bit older, I went through a PBS phase (mostly because we didn't get Disney or Nickelodeon in my old house; I was stuck with the basic channels until we eventually moved). These days, my favorite shows air on Disney XD and the Cartoon Network. And *of course* I still have favorite cartoons, even though I am now a teenager. I will never outgrow them! I swear, I'll still be obsessed with cartoons when I'm fifty.

So, why am I telling you all this? Because I want to tell you about something amazing that happened when I was only about four years old. I was watching Playhouse Disney, and during the commercial break I caught a short segment, just a little two-minute featurette before the next program started, about interesting and unusual jobs. Rather than careers that even super-young kids are familiar with, like doctor or firefighter or policewoman, this program highlighted jobs that children might not even know existed. I'd never seen the special before (it was only later that I found out it was an ongoing series), and I've never seen an episode since. Maybe it was fate, then, that the one airing I managed to see was all about the people who made the very cartoons I loved so much—the show was about professional animators.

For the first time, it occurred to me that the cartoons I watched every morning weren't actually about real, live people. I mean, I knew they weren't *real*—I understood that SpongeBob didn't *actually* live in a pineapple under the sea; I knew that there wasn't *actually* a city called

Bikini Bottom at the bottom of the ocean—but in terms of understanding, I was still in a kind of murky in-between. Even though I often drew the characters I loved to watch, and even though I sometimes invented my own (like the Barking Brothers), it still seemed like something totally magical was happening on the television. That's the only way I can really explain it. In terms of how my favorite cartoons actually made it onto the screen, I just hadn't given it any more thought than that.

Now, for some kids, the realization that SpongeBob isn't an actual walking, talking sponge with legs—the knowledge that there's someone behind the scenes drawing and animating and even voicing the character—might ruin some of that magic. But for me, this awakening made the cartoons I loved even more special. It meant that I could create those exciting adventures and unique, imaginative worlds, too. I'd had no idea that there were people out there who made cartoons for a living, but right then and there, I knew what I wanted to do with the rest of my life. "That's what I want to be," I said (although I can't remember if I actually said this out loud, or if the thought just echoed in my head). One thing was for sure: I was going to become a professional animator.

My creative journey could've ended right there, but I was lucky to have parents who encouraged me to pursue *all* my creative ideas, to run with my instincts 24/7. (I've also always been something of a Flip-Flopper, someone who flits from one idea to the next rather quickly—but more on that in a bit.)

One afternoon, around the same time I was discovering my passion for animation, my dad called me in to his office to see if I wanted to watch him take apart his computer. He's always doing stuff like this, by the way. My dad's a pretty tech-savvy guy, and he usually prefers to fix things himself rather than take his electronics in to get serviced. (Not too long ago, for example, he took his cell phone apart, too.) On this particular afternoon, he wanted to blast the insides of his computer with a can of compressed air; by cleaning the parts, he was trying to get the thing to run a bit faster.

Back then—as I mentioned, I was only about four years old—I didn't really know all that much about computers. I knew they were machines, that they were gadgets of sorts; I understood them mostly as something you could do "work" on. I think I might've even likened computers to robots. So I had no idea just how complex the innards of a computer were until my dad took off the cover of the CPU tower. And even though I didn't understand anything he was showing me (he pointed out the motherboard and various microchips), I thought what he was doing was really, really cool. It spawned an interest in (and eventually a love for) technology. I didn't yet realize the ways that my new love of tech would one day merge with my already established love of art, but it would.

Around age seven or eight, I discovered yet another interest, something else I wanted to learn more about. On occasion, I'd notice my mother mending the hem of a shirt or darning a sock. She didn't sew a lot, but I remember feeling sort of wowed nonetheless. I remember thinking, *My mom is so awesome, she can make and fix literally anything!* I wanted to make things, too. Specifically, I wanted to try my hand at making my own stuffed animals. So I finally asked her to teach me. I was pleased to discover that the basics of sewing came pretty easily, although for some reason I had a lot of trouble tying a knot in the string after threading the needle. (But shhh! Please don't tell anyone that. I must maintain my reputation as a sewing ninja.)

The first thing I created was a plush cat made out of pink and green fabric. I named her Watermelon. To be honest, she was anything but beautiful—you could see the stuffing coming out of her seams. In fact, she was kind of a mess. But I still was proud, and I still have her. As I write this, Watermelon is somewhere in my room, chilling out.

After that, my interest in sewing kind of took off and I began to make whatever idea popped into my head. My parents are hardworking folks, but they didn't have tons of extra money, so I mostly used vintage or recycled fabrics I found around the house, like discarded swatches, leftover felt, or cast-off ribbon. And either because they weren't too difficult to make or because I just wanted something to put in my hair, I started experimenting with crafting cloth-style headbands, the kind you tie at the nape of your neck.

I still remember the first two I made: one was made out of blue ribbon, onto which I sewed a yellow flower appliqué; the other was orange, with an orange-and-blue flower. To my delight, they were pretty darn cute. Totally cute enough to actually wear out in public. So I'd wrap one around my hair and head out to the grocery store or to church or wherever.

At that point, sewing and making headbands was just a hobby—not like animation, which I knew I wanted to pursue professionally one day. But I quickly started getting compliments on my creations, first from family and friends, and then from total strangers. I'd be standing in line at the grocery store, and the cashier might say, "Oh, what a cute headband. Where can I get one?" Or a woman at church might ask, "Do you have any more of those for sale?" I'd always smile and say something like, "Maybe someday!" At that age, it just hadn't occurred to me that a kid could sell his or her creations.

All of that changed, however, when I discovered a website called Etsy.

My mom was on the computer, scrolling through pictures of jewelry, scarves, and antiquey-looking knickknacks. When I asked what she was looking at, she explained that the website—Etsy.com—was a place to buy handmade and vintage items online.

These days, Etsy is a super-popular e-commerce site (with more than fifty million users!), but back then it was only a couple of years old. In fact, online shopping in general wasn't nearly as popular as it is now, and I hadn't even really grasped the concept that it was *possible* to sell things online. (I might've had a growing interest in technology, but most of what I knew about the Internet extended to "Don't talk to strangers online" and "Don't tell people your name or give out your address.") I always thought that to sell stuff—to run a business—you had to have an actual, physical brick-and-mortar store. So when people asked where they might be able to buy my headbands, that's probably what I pictured in my head: a physical location. And that just wouldn't be possible for an eight-year-old kid. I mean, how was I supposed to buy a whole building? Would I have to, I don't know, *hire a construction crew?*

When I saw the website, though, something clicked: I realized that I didn't have to have a physical brick-and-mortar store. And I certainly didn't have to hire a construction crew. All at once, I saw a way for the interests and passions I'd been cultivating—my love for drawing and designing, my growing interest in tech, and my sewing and crafting hobby—to come together. In a flash, I had that Big Idea. I was going to start my own business.

Truth be told, it wasn't the first time I'd tried running my own company. As a little kid, I briefly had a "store" that I ran out of my bedroom, selling plastic pizzas to all my stuffed animals. Back when I was still a toddler, and still eating my meals in a high chair, I owned and operated a very special "restaurant." The special of the day, if you're wondering, was something called snake soup, a carefully crafted blend of water, ketchup, dried beans, and a plastic snake toy. It was pretend culinary goodness.

This, however, was different. I wasn't just playing around anymore. I was serious.

I might have been lacking in experience, and I might've had the fashion sense of, well, an eight-year-old, but I wasn't going to let that stop me! I was going to launch an actual, viable clothing company, and it was going to be *awesome*.

THE BIG QUESTION:
WHAT WILL I DO WITH MY LIFE?

Not all girls know what they want to do with their life by the ripe old age of four. And not everyone starts a business at eight. But I'll bet that, even if you have no idea what you might like to do, you've probably asked yourself—or someone *else* has asked you—the question. Probably the first time when you were still teeny-tiny. And it probably went a little like this:

KIND, SMILING, SPEAKING-IN-A-BABY-VOICE ADULT: So, [insert your name here], what do you want to be when you grow up?

TEENY-TINY, GRINNING EAR-TO-EAR YOU: A firefighter! [Or a superhero, singer, doctor, dancer, candy store owner, and/or lion tamer.]

Of course, at some point you probably realized that becoming a combination veterinarian–movie star–Olympic athlete wasn't exactly a *practical* choice. I mean, sure, there are a handful of people out there who seemingly always knew what they were put on this earth to do—the NBA forward who was practically born with a basketball in hand, the concert violinist who begged for music lessons before she started kindergarten, the pediatrician who began his medical training by monitoring his stuffed animals with a plastic stethoscope. For most of us, though, it takes much longer to find a path forward. And the older you get, the more you begin to turn those questions over and over again in your mind: "What *do* I want to be? What *do* I want to do with my life? And *how on earth* will I do it?" Some people (especially Under-Thinkers) can even become distressed at not knowing the answers. It can be incredibly daunting, particularly when you're still in your tweens and teens, to envision a life that's full and influential and meaningful.

But here's the good news: you might *already* be figuring out your future, maybe without even realizing it.

Do you take your "fun" seriously? Let me explain what I mean by that. There's a saying by child development experts that "play is children's work," meaning that play—building with blocks, solving puzzles, reading stories, or coloring in coloring books—helps kids develop the social, physical, and emotional skills they'll need to become happy, successful grown-ups. For little kids, playtime isn't just important; it's vital. But I think playtime is just as necessary for older kids and teens, too, because one of the most important aspects of play is that it nurtures our innate creativity—it stimulates the *creative mind*.

Creativity has always been a major part of my life, even when I was still knee-high to a grasshopper. From those earliest doodles to the way I arranged tater tots on a plate (usually half covered in ketchup and half not, stacked up into some kind of teetering tower or shape), I've always tried to do things in unique and creative ways. Now, I'm not saying that's always been easy. Some days, it seems as though finding the motivation to be creative would require going on a long trek up the mystical Mountain of Ideas on the one thousandth year of the full moon, and waiting for the magic portal to the Valley of Inspiration to open up (or, er, something like that). And yet, whenever I experience a *lack* of creativity, I feel thirstier than when I have a lack of water. Maybe that's because creativity isn't just instinctual, it's *spiritual*.

For example, I never got to meet my aunt Lisa, because she passed away before I was born. I know that she was a very talented artist and painter, though, and I keep a picture of her in my room. Through creative expression, I can feel her presence. I feel as though whenever I draw or paint, I'm having a conversation with her. I feel like she lives on through me and my passion for art.

Inspiration (which I like to think of as creativity's cousin) can also be an elusive, mysterious, or even mystical thing. After all, inspiration is that moment when a creative spark presents itself to you seemingly out of nowhere. It can reveal itself slowly, or progress quickly. It can strike when you're in a quiet space or in the middle of a loud crowd. During happy times or sad. It's never expected. Never predicted. But should always be welcomed. Inspiration is that thing that propels you to create, to feel, to act on a sudden idea or thought process. But you don't have to take my word for it. Here's how Beethoven, the great composer, described it: "I call inspiration that mysterious state in which the entire world seems to form a vast harmony, when every sentiment, every thought, re-echoes within me, when all the forces of Nature become instruments to me, when my whole body shivers and my hair stands on end."

So that moment when a thought pops into your head completely out of the blue, when inspiration strikes, when your hair stands on end? That's the work of your creative mind.

But, wait. Let's back up for a minute. What do I *really* mean by "creativity"? That you can draw or sculpt or take amazing photographs? That you can whip up just about anything with a needle and thread, or pick up a guitar and pluck out a tune? Sure, all those things are wonderfully creative, but when I talk about creativity, I don't just mean things you can accomplish with a hot glue gun or by filling a blank canvas. Creativity can also be expressed through creative thinking and creative problem solving.

For example, not long after launching my company (and we'll talk more about that in part II), I started dreaming of having my own website. I did some research online and came across lots of website-building platforms, but none of them were as customizable as I'd hoped. I also didn't want to pay for a membership to any of those platforms, which would've been necessary to unlock the customization tools. So what did I do? I Googled "how to make my own website from scratch" (or something like that). And that's when I came across something called HTML.

HTML, as you may know, stands for HyperText Markup Language; it's one of the many "languages" that are used to speak to computers, and it's used in a lot of website building. Now, learning code isn't exactly a walk in the park. In fact, it can be just as difficult as learning a human language, like French, Spanish, or Mandarin. But I was only ten at the time (I didn't really know what I was getting myself into), so I decided that I'd just teach myself as much as I could about HTML in order to build my own website. Before long, I'd learned enough to be able to write some lines of code in Notepad (that program you'll find preinstalled on any Windows computer), and after a quick test run in my browser, it worked!

The point is, being creative doesn't just mean that you're *artistically* inclined. In my case, I wanted to do something to improve and grow my business, and I didn't want to have to spend any money to do it. Teaching myself HTML was a creative way of solving a problem.

Speaking of "solving a problem," that's probably what prompted a fifteen-year-old named Chester Greenwood to invent earmuffs way back in the 1800s. (The problem he was solving? Cold ears, of course!) It's certainly what inspired Krysta Morlan, a high school student, to invent something called the "Cast Cooler," a device for keeping a broken arm or leg cool and comfortable while encased in a healing (yet often hot, itchy, uncomfortable) cast. Did you know that Braille, the reading and writing system for the blind and visually impaired, was invented by Louis Braille when he was still just a kid?

There are a zillion people out there who can't carry a tune or draw a bowl of fruit, but who are just as creative as any artist ever born. It's how you express that creativity— whether through singing or drawing or inventing a machine or solving a problem—that makes each of us special and unique. In other words, your creativity is what makes you *awesome*.

So now that we've got a handle on what creativity is, how do we start to tap into it?

The great thing about creativity (in all its forms) is that creative impulses are generally fun impulses. If you have a creative idea, chances are it's to make something or do something that you and others will enjoy. It's positive and upbeat—it's fun.

Think about it: my interest in art and animation didn't have anything to do with seeking out a future career path. I was interested in both things for no other reason than that they were fun! (So fun, in fact, that I recently took some summer animation classes at the Savannah College of Art and Design; I continue to work on the craft both as part of my schoolwork and during my free time.) Likewise, my interest in designing and making headbands was based solely on the fact that it was something I genuinely enjoyed; I just happened to be able to turn that love into a business. What motivation other than "fun" could there have been for the person who created the first popsicle (an eleven-year-old named Frank Epperson, by the way)? Or the trampoline (a sixteen-year-old named George Nissen)? Some truly fun—not to mention amazing—inventions have come from the minds of kids. After all, most kids have a natural desire to play, experiment, and explore. Sometimes what we like to "play" can actually become our work, our career, our future.

The trouble starts when we're made to believe that our crazy, silly, fun ideas aren't serious. As we get older, we sometimes fall into a trap of believing that our imaginative ideas are immature. We start to confuse child*like* fun with being child*ish*. We tell ourselves that it's time to buckle down and get serious. We start to shut those creative impulses down.

But if we ignore the ideas that spring from the fun part of our brain, we may forgo some valuable contributions to the world. Just think what we'd be missing if Steve Jobs had said to himself, "A phone with a computer screen that you carry around in your pocket? *That's* a silly idea." Where would we be if J. K. Rowling had never imagined writing about a boy wizard named Harry who studied magic (or if she had had the idea but never pursued it)?

For example, maybe you've always loved the ocean. Maybe you've obsessively read about life underwater since you were a kid. Maybe Sebastian, the talking crab from *The Little Mermaid*, is your spirit animal. Maybe you've started creating these funny (to you, anyway) animations of crazy sea creature encounters—dolphin vs. clown fish! Is this really just wasting time? What if your talking turtles, whales, and plankton are the beginning of a career writing children's books, or—like me—you have an interest in animation? Perhaps you're curious about deep-sea photography or filmmaking, like the great Jacques Cousteau? Or maybe you'll go on to study oceanography, invent a way to clean up oil spills, or fight beach erosion?

Or, maybe you're fascinated by makeup. Every spare cent you earn from babysitting or from your first part-time job goes toward the newest blushes, lipsticks, and illuminating creams. You're a master of the cat eye. You can contour as good as the pros. You live for makeup, but you don't really share that love with anyone, since some of your friends think your obsession is silly. Your mom might even ask, "Honey, why are you spending so much time thinking about *eye shadow*?"

But maybe your love of long lashes could turn into a whole website devoted to makeup reviews? And maybe those reviews get the attention of thousands of readers, not to mention most of the major cosmetics companies?

Your creativity is a gift. So don't ignore your creative impulses, even if they seem silly or childish. Pay attention to your play. Take your fun seriously. Who knows? You could be doing something "just for fun" that could mark the beginning of a career path.

FLIP-FLOPPERS, BLANK-DRAWERS, AND UNDER-THINKERS: WHICH ONE ARE YOU?

It's totally fine if you don't yet know what you want to do with your life, especially if you're just now beginning to ponder the possibilities. So take a break from worrying about *that* question, and try answering this one instead: "How do I make decisions about my life?" I'll bet that, like most people (me included), you fall into one of the following categories:

The Flip-Flopper

If there's one thing the Flip-Flopper doesn't lack, it's ideas. You've got lots of interests and passions, tons of things you want to accomplish. The problem? Sometimes it feels like you have *too many* career goals. Your aspirations can change in an instant:

> *Hmmm . . . I love pizza. Maybe I want to be a pizza chef and open a restaurant one day. Or, I could become a food critic—I'll write about the best dishes at restaurants all over town! Or a cookbook author? I'll teach other people to make tasty meals. But I also love electronics and technology . . . maybe I'll build a robot that makes pizza?!*

On the one hand, having more than one vision for your future isn't exactly a bad thing. Since you're able to see an abundance of possibilities, you'll likely be able to create an abundance of opportunities for yourself. On the other hand, Flip-Floppers tend to flit from one idea to the next really quickly, often with little to no follow-through. Ironically, the Flip-Flopper's lack of focus can prevent her from getting anything done at all.

I can relate: I am mostly a Flip-Flopper (although I've definitely got some Blank-Drawer and Under-Thinker tendencies, too). After all, I'm an artist, an animator, an eco-friendly fashion designer, an entrepreneur, a coder, a philanthropist, a writer, and a motivational speaker—that's a lot of balls to have in the air all at once! It *is* possible to pursue all of your passions, though, without getting too sidetracked or overwhelmed in the process. The key is to focus on just one thing at a time. For example, I choose *one* thing to pour my energy into—like starting my business, Maya's Ideas—and work on it until it feels sustainable. Only then do I take on a new project. In contrast, had I tried to launch a nonprofit organization at the same time I was starting my for-profit business, I'd be more all over the place than I am now (not to mention plain exhausted)!

Like any Flip-Flopper, I've still got tons of ideas that I haven't made any headway on yet. Another way I stay focused is by stashing those ideas in the "concept vault." That way, I don't have to worry about losing them; I'm free to get back to them when the time is right. If you're a Flip-Flopper, pay special attention to the section "Creating a Concept Vault" on page 57. That's where I'll teach you how to make your own concept vault (a.k.a. an Idea Book), which will help you slow down, process, and organize all your amazing ideas, and choose which ones you most want to pursue.

The Blank-Drawer

If the Flip-Flopper sees too many possibilities out there, the Blank-Drawer just isn't seeing enough. You have the drive, you know you want to do something meaningful, but every time you're asked that magic question—"What do you want to do with your life?"—you draw a blank. Sound familiar?

In my experience, Blank-Drawers tend to be very passionate individuals—they think of their time and talents as extremely important resources, and they absolutely refuse to waste any energy pursuing a goal that doesn't impress, inspire, or move them. In fact, Blank-Drawers often know more about what they *don't* like than what they do. For example, you may love art and art history, but you're not great at drawing or painting, you don't want to be a teacher, and you find museums to be stuffy and boring—so working at one is out, too. Or, you're passionate about nature and the environment, but you can't picture yourself working as a scientist, or an engineer, or an activist. Blank-Drawers are often very picky when it comes to crafting their future.

Now, this pickiness has some definite pros. On the upside, Blank-Drawers tend to be extremely ambitious people. As soon as they find their "something," they focus on it 100 percent. Blank-Drawers are often great at time management, too. (After all, the last thing a Blank-Drawer wants to do is drain her time and talents on something that isn't truly "worth it" or meaningful.)

But there's a downside to being *so* sure about what you like and don't like, especially at such a young age: you may wind up limiting yourself. You might miss opportunities that you didn't even know existed because you were too afraid or stubborn or reluctant to explore. It's great to be focused, but by trying new things (even when you think you might not get anything out of it in the long run), you still gain valuable experience and grow as a person.

If you're a Blank-Drawer, make sure to check out the sections "Creativity + Curiosity = Your Awesomeness, Unleashed" on page 43, and "Busting Out of Your Comfort Zone" on page 53—these will help you expand your horizons, encourage you to explore and experiment, and help you determine whether what you *think* you know about yourself is really actually true.

The Under-Thinker

The Under-Thinker isn't changing her mind every day, flitting from one idea to the next like the Flip-Flopper. And she's not as picky as the Blank-Drawer. When it comes to answering that all-important question—"What do you want to do with your life?"—the Under-Thinker just hasn't thought about it yet. Instead, she's focused on the basics, like acing that math test, winning that soccer game, or making toast without setting the kitchen on fire. The future? For the Under-Thinker, that's a looong way off.

Lots of people, young and old, don't give the future a whole lot of thought, because they're focused on the here and now; they're living in the present. And while there are some benefits to being in-the-moment (Under-Thinkers almost always take time to stop and smell the roses, so to speak), the problem with this approach is that by ignoring your future—by refusing to think about it—you could be ignoring your potential, too.

Let's take a look at the reasons why you aren't thinking about tomorrow. Perhaps you feel discouraged? Maybe you've been criticized in the past:

What do you mean you don't have a clue about what you'd like to do? You should really have some ideas by now! What have you been spending all your time doing?!

That kind of criticism is not only hurtful; it can paralyze you with fear. (*Maybe my parents/teachers/coaches are right. Look at* [insert name of successful friend here]. *She's so far ahead of me in figuring out this stuff!*) Sometimes the way we cope with that fear is to shut down, to just under-think the whole thing, to forget about and ignore the possibilities.

Listen up: You are not alone. There are a zillion Under-Thinkers out there, and many of them have gone on to achieve great things. So don't listen to the little voice in your head that says there's something wrong with you for not knowing what your goals are yet. (That little voice, by the way, could be your own voice, or it could be someone else's, even someone you love and respect—like your mom or dad—who's just worried about your future, too.) All you need is a little help getting pointed in the right direction.

If you're an Under-Thinker, you'll want to focus on the next section in this book, "How a Dream Board Can Help You Dream Big" (page 31), which will help you discover your passions naturally, without putting so much pressure on yourself.

HOW A DREAM BOARD
CAN HELP YOU DREAM BIG

Zeroing In on What Makes You Awesome

When I was little and my parents didn't feel like cooking dinner, they'd sometimes send out for sushi. I didn't like sushi back then (I guess I didn't have a sophisticated enough palette—I love it now!), so instead of raw fish, I'd eat a fortune cookie.

The cookies were okay—a little dry, a little bland—but what I really liked were the fortunes, particularly the positive ones that promised you "peace and happiness in the coming years," stuff like that. It was like getting a magical message written just for you. They reminded me of sacred scrolls, just big enough (or tiny enough) for a mouse. On one particular evening, I got a fortune that really spoke to me. I don't remember what it said anymore (something generic about prosperity and happiness, probably); I might have even just liked the fact that it had smiley faces on it. All I know is that it made me feel like something good might happen or like luck might come my way. So I grabbed some Scotch tape (knowing me, it was probably just lying around my room, left over from a previous craft project) and taped the fortune on the wall next to my bed. That way, I'd see it when I said my prayers at night.

I've always lived in a faith-based household. My parents instilled in me that it's important to be grateful and grounded (not "grounded" like stuck in your room, but rather stable, secure, and well balanced). My mother taught me all about meditation, and we sometimes listened to motivational speakers like Dr. Wayne Dyer. We even do yoga in the mornings, which is a great way to unwind when things in your life start to get crazy. Because of all those things, I started focusing on being positive from a very young age. I understood the benefit of surrounding yourself with positive affirmations and messages—even in the form of great fortunes from fortune cookies.

Not long after taping that first fortune to the side of my

bed, I started taping new ones (as well as other kinds of positive messages, including inspirational sayings and quotes) in other places: next to my light switch—so that every time I entered my room, I'd be greeted by a burst of positivity—on the wall, anywhere I might see them throughout the day, not just when I was going to sleep at night.

Fast-forward to age seven or eight, and I had decided to take that positivity to the next level. I was ready to create my own "dream board," filled with uplifting fortunes, drawings, illustrations, and quotes. (Although it wasn't actually a "board"—it was just a sheet of colored construction paper.) I cut out pictures from magazines, two dogs from the cardboard sleeve of the straight-to-DVD movie *Air Buddies* (mostly because I desperately wanted a pet), even the logo from a macaroni-and-cheese box. (I eat a lot of snacks made by a company called Annie's. The corporate logo is a rabbit; I particularly like the Peace, Pasta, and Parmesan macaroni and cheese because the pasta is made in the shape of peace signs and the rabbit is wearing a tie-dyed shirt on the box. Who says mac and cheese isn't positive?) Underneath all those pictures and cardboard cutouts, I wrote inspirational words and sayings, like "believe," "put on a happy face," "friendship," and "make the world a better place." Anytime I was feeling down about whatever crisis was going on in my seven-year-old world (which admittedly couldn't have been *that* big a deal, since my primary concerns were probably Legos and the shows on PBS Kids), I would turn to that dream board, and, like magic, it would make me feel better. I still have it, in fact, tucked into an old portfolio. Now that I'm a teenager, it looks a little bit cheesy and childish, but it still never fails to put a smile on my face.

By the time I turned eleven, I'd already launched my business and I was beginning to see the world through a bigger lens. I had started to think about the people, places, and things that gave me hope for the future or sparked my creative drive. That's when I took notice of a certain wall in my studio (the room where I make everything that I sell via Maya's Ideas). That wall was the first thing I saw every day when I came in and sat down to work—it set the tone for my whole workspace, in fact—but it was just a blank, bare white wall. It was practically screaming for some life, some kind of decoration. And then it hit me: I would make a whole wall of inspiration, not just a board. With my parents' okay, I took over the space.

Ever since making my wall of inspiration, the whole

tone of my studio has changed. It's brighter and much more creative, which was the whole point of having a studio in the first place! Here's what you'll find on my dream board (er, inspiration wall) these days: My grandmother used to tell me, "Maya, with God all things are possible," and that quote became a kind of overarching theme; I printed it out and tacked it right at the top. Below that, I've got pictures of Rosa Parks, because she gives me a boost of courage whenever I need it; Gabby Douglas, the Olympic gymnast who energizes and inspires me to push myself just a little bit harder; and Gabrielle Bernstein, a wonderful and inspiring speaker, author, and all-around guru who lifts me up and is an embodiment of all things positive. I've also got pictures of my family members, and some funny photos of my pets (including my dog, Blackberry, and my two cats, Coconut and Fritter). You'll also see lots of stuff about art, including one of my favorite photos ever taken, a shot of me standing next to Vincent van Gogh's famous painting *Starry Night*.

I first saw the painting when I was only a year or two old, in a *Baby Einstein* video featuring the one and only Vincent van Goat (yes, a goat puppet). Many years later, I was headed to New York City and the world-famous

Museum of Modern Art—since I'm homeschooled, my parents are in charge of the field trips—and I just *had* to see the real thing. It was awe inspiring, of course, a truly incredible thing to see up close and in person, but what I really wanted was a picture of myself next to the painting. Now, the museum doesn't exactly encourage this kind of thing, but the security guard on duty was nice enough to let me take one. Whenever I look at that picture, I'm inspired not just by the power of Van Gogh's work, but by the memory of a stranger who treated my family with such kindness. It's something I'll treasure forever.

Dream boards (or vision boards or inspiration walls, whatever you want to call them) are great because they provide a visual source of inspiration. Whenever I feel down, discouraged, or creatively stuck, I literally stare at the wall in my studio for a boost of confidence or a shot of encouragement, or to lift my spirits. But dream boards are *also* great because they can help us zero in on what we're truly passionate about. Making a dream board can help you tap into your raw creative energy.

Sometimes the hardest part about figuring out your future is just getting started. After all, saying to yourself, "I need to figure out what I want to do for the next fifty years of my life" can be a little daunting, so let's take it down a notch. Just for a moment, forget about your future. Don't worry about what you want to be doing five, twenty, or fifty years from now. This is about having fun. (Creative impulses, remember, are generally fun impulses.) Whether you have a vague idea of what you want to do or absolutely no idea—and I'm talking to you, Under-Thinkers!—this exercise will help you out.

MAKE YOUR OWN DREAM BOARD

What you'll need: Magazines, postcards, newspapers, or photographs (so long as you've got the okay to cut them up); scissors; glue or tape; and an open mind.

Making a dream board is a little different from starting a scrapbook or thumbtacking party pics and ticket stubs to your bulletin board. That's not to say that your first-prize ribbon from the swim meet shouldn't make the cut if it's a source of encouragement. Ditto for that boarding pass from a recent plane trip or that program from a special performance or show. But the goal here is looking ahead, not back. A dream board should be less about what you *have* done and more about what you're *into*. Here's what to do:

Start Small. You don't have to dedicate an entire wall to your dreams (although if you want to, go for it). Just remember that you can make a great dream board on a small piece of poster board. I started with a single sheet of construction paper.

Don't Worry, Be Happy. If the characters on the mac-and-cheese box make you smile, use 'em. Or, if mac and cheese doesn't do it for you, try flipping through old magazines or your favorite books for inspiration. What brings you the most joy could be a simple snapshot with friends or a great vacation photo, a postcard of a place you'd like to visit one day, art from your favorite artist, a funny joke your brother told you, even a printout of the funniest (in your opinion) emojis. Do you love volleyball? Maybe paste up a picture of you with your volleyball teammates, or slap a sticker of a volleyball next to your favorite inspirational quote. You're going for anything that brings you positivity and light, but the point is to *not* overthink things. If it passes the happy test—even if you can't really explain why—it goes on the board.

> **Leave It Unfinished.** Huh? Aren't you always supposed to finish what you start? Well, in this case it's okay—preferable, even—not to finish the project. After all, if your day-to-day life is still changing and taking shape, so, too, is your future. You may find that as you grow, so do your dreams (and, therefore, so does your board).

Did you make your dream board yet?

Yes?

Okay, good. You're ready to continue on to the next part.

I've already told you what's on my wall, but if I were to stand back and analyze it—if I were to search it for themes—here's what I'd see: lots of pictures of strong and powerful women, lots of pictures of animals and of nature (trees, flowers, lakes, and streams), and representations of art in all its forms. Which makes sense when you think about it, doesn't it? Some of my primary interests and passions include women and girls' rights (we'll talk more about that in part III), the environment and sustainability (remember, I run an eco-friendly fashion company), and art, which, as I think I've made clear, is my primary love.

Analyzing your dream board for common themes—or clues, if you will—can be helpful when you're trying to find your path, when you're attempting to discern what matters to you most. So, I want you to take a step back and look at your dream board. What jumps out?

Maybe you posted lots of pictures of Paris and all things Parisian—the Eiffel Tower, a woman wearing a red beret, a postcard of a bridge spanning the Seine. Hmm . . . what is it about Paris that prompted you to cut out so many pictures? It could be that you love the sound of French, that you're interested in learning to speak another language. Or, maybe your favorite restaurant is a French restaurant, and you'd like to know more about French food. Maybe you just want to travel the world someday.

Or, perhaps you pasted up lots of images from popular movies. But what is it about movies that sucks you in? Are those movies animated or live action? Do you like the performance aspect, or is it the stories themselves that move you? Perhaps they're all science fiction films, and what you're really interested in is technology, or robotics, or artificial intelligence.

Keep exploring your dream board for clues and common themes, even if you don't recognize any right away. What you love is probably staring you right in the face!

CREATIVITY + CURIOSITY = YOUR AWESOMENESS, UNLEASHED

By now, we've talked about taking your fun seriously and zeroing in on your passions by making a dream board—we've given your creative mind a bit of a workout. But there's another component to unleashing your awesomeness that I want to talk about, too.

Not too long ago, I was doing an interview. About halfway through, the reporter stopped to pay me a compliment. "You must be really smart to have accomplished so much at such a young age," she said. And that got me thinking, what does it mean to be "smart"?

Does smart mean that you get straight As every semester, or that you're first to solve a problem, to raise your hand with the right answer? Sure, that can totally mean

that you're smart—in fact, we normally call those kinds of skills "book smarts." But being smart isn't always just about grades. It's important to get an education, of course, and it's certainly not okay to slack off in school. You should always, always try your best. But I don't think kids and teens should let just their grades define them. There are lots of really, really smart people who didn't or don't perform all that well in school.

What other words could we use to stand in for "smart"? "Intelligent," "quick-witted," and "wise" come to mind. But what about . . . "curious"? Isn't curiosity the very thing that drives you to learn more, to ask questions, to gain knowledge, and to try new things?

After all, I might have started designing and making headbands for *fun*, but I started my company out of *curiosity*. Since it had never before occurred to me that a kid could run a business, I wanted to understand how it all worked. The initial steps to launching Maya's Ideas, in fact, were largely centered on learning more about Etsy.

Curiosity is also what drove me to learn more about animation. I didn't realize it then, but in a way—even before watching that two-minute Playhouse Disney television special—I had long been trying my hand at making cartoons. For example, *Stuart Little 2* was one of my absolute favorite movies when I was younger. I'd watch it over and over and over again. (I'm not sure why I liked the second one so much better than the first, but I could recall the whole thing for you right now if you wanted.) Then I'd sit down, grab a sketchbook, and draw each and every significant scene, one right after the other, kind of like storyboarding. Of course, I rarely made it all the way to the end of the movie—I'd get tired of drawing the same thing over and over—but this was kind of like my way of trying to animate. I just didn't know how to make those characters *move*.

When I got a little older—this is after I saw the Playhouse Disney special—I wanted to learn everything I possibly could about animation; I wanted to understand how it actually worked. I watched tons of YouTube clips and tutorials (a great source of information for learning more about . . . well, almost anything). I also learned more than I could have imagined just by paying closer attention to my favorite movies. Whenever I got a new DVD of an animated film, I'd head straight for the behind-the-scenes footage. Over time, I became familiar with all the major styles and techniques: 2-D, 3-D, stop-motion (like *Coraline* or *The Nightmare Before Christmas*), and Claymation (like the *Wallace and Gromit* cartoons).

Since my dad knew how much I loved animation, and also how much time I'd spent learning about it, he got me an intro-to-animation computer program for kids when I was around eight years old. He also gave me my first digital drawing tablet, let me borrow his old MacBook, and installed all the software for me. The program was easy to learn—a great teaching tool for me at the time—and helped me grasp how basic animation worked.

Obviously, none of my original animations were super-full-blown cartoons. I was mostly trying to master small movements—not even as advanced as getting a character to walk across the screen or move his mouth in time to dialogue, more like getting him to wave or jump in the air, just basic stuff like that. Eventually, though, I was able to make my first digital short, a thirty-second clip about my pet cat fighting a toy mouse that I'd left lying around on the floor of my room. (Except they were ninjas. I called it *Ninja Kooky*, because Kooky is a nickname I sometimes use for my cat Coconut.) Little did I know I'd later showcase my animations when I did my first TED talk, premiering my creations on a global stage.

Back when I was four or five, I could have just said, *I like cartoons; I'd like to do that someday.* But by educating myself—by being curious—I didn't just learn about animation, I *did* it. By eight years old, I was able to create my own cartoons.

❧❀❧

Now I want you to take another look at that dream board. You may have already identified the broad themes, you may have already pinpointed some general interests, but what makes you genuinely curious? What might you learn more about?

For example, maybe your dream board is filled with images from your favorite movies because you dream of one day becoming an actor. Have you ever actually given it a shot? Ever acted in an actual play? Is there a community theater in your area? Acting classes in your city? A drama program you can join at your school?

Or perhaps you posted a lot of postcards from foreign, exotic places, because what you really love is photography. Do you know how to check your camera's aperture (or f-stop) setting? Do you know which chemicals are used in photo processing? Ever been inside an actual darkroom?

All of those questions provide a way forward, a way to start turning your passions into actions, and there are a ton of ways to learn more about all the things that you love: Internet research, YouTube tutorials, television shows and documentaries (even the behind-the-scenes footage from your favorite movies), educational programs or summer camps, local book clubs or sports leagues or theater troupes you could join. (If there isn't a club or a group in your area, perhaps you could start one.)

Success isn't really based on how smart a person is—lots of kids (and adults, too) are plenty smart, have really great ideas, and are in tune with their creative mind. Success is much more closely linked to taking that next step, to educating yourself and exploring, to being curious.

WHAT IF NOTHING ON MY DREAM BOARD JUMPS OUT?

So, you're gazing at your dream board and—to your horror—it looks like a jumbled mess. You've got a postcard from London up there, a magazine article about surfing, a dried flower from the garden, screenshots from *The Lego Movie*, a quote about courage, and a lot of pictures of *strawberries* . . . for some strange reason. You have no idea what any of this means; you can't find any themes or common ground. Now what?

If themes or interests or passions don't pop out from your dream board right away, don't worry. We all feel a little foggy sometimes, or distracted or out of touch with our creative mind. People sometimes forget, though, that creativity (as well as your ability to recognize creative impulses when you have them) is something you can improve upon, something you can get better at, just like any other skill. Sometimes that takes practice, and sometimes what your mind needs is a bit of a break. When I get a little stuck or my ideas feel stale, I do a few things to recharge my batteries:

Unplug. I love technology in all its forms. I'm fascinated by it. But the truth is that tech and social media are kind of like the elephant in the room for our generation— whether we admit it or not, we all know that we're probably spending a little too much time on our phones, online, on Facebook, watching TV, or scrolling through the videos on YouTube. So, hard as it is, I purposely set aside some time each week to step away from the texts, the emails, and the computer holding all my work files. I leave my studio and go outside to walk or run or meditate, or I play with my dog or hang with a friend or paint or read or sometimes just wander into the other room to see what my mom is up to. Even when I'm really busy or up against a crazy deadline, I feel much more fresh and productive and creative when I allow myself to take an occasional break.

Eliminate the Negative. If too much exposure to technology is the elephant in the room for our generation, then it goes without saying that we're all exposed to various kinds of media. The problem is that sometimes magazines, television shows, music videos, and even our friends' Facebook pages can send subliminal messages about how we should act, dress, feel, or think. Media can make us feel as though we're not quite—or we'll never be—hip or cool enough. Sometimes it's healthy to take a break from all that, especially if certain kinds of media make you feel down.

For example, you might want to periodically clean up your Instagram feed, especially if you're seeing a lot of negative posts or fads. If whenever you look at your Facebook timeline you're inundated with negativity, perhaps it's time to hit that magic Unfriend button. You can also make an effort to start following or friending more positive, uplifting people and pages. You want to feel inspired when you read or watch television or check into your social media accounts, not depressed. The good news is that we have much more control over the media—and the things we allow to influence us—than we realize. So get rid of the negative.

Be Bored. Being bored is kind of like unplugging, except instead of taking a break to do something fun, I purposely set out to do something kind of *dull*, like running an errand I've been putting off or doing a chore like folding laundry. I often find that doing boring, minimally stimulating tasks gives my mind a chance to wander and daydream—which just happens to be when I get some of my best ideas. As it turns out, boredom is a great motivator!

BUSTING OUT OF
YOUR COMFORT ZONE

While you're perusing your dream board and taking notes (either mental or actual) on what you might like to learn more about, I'd like you to take a moment to list some skills or hobbies that you're *not* good at, that you *aren't* interested in, too. That goes double for all you Blank-Drawers.

Let's say you're really not into drawing. You're no good at it. You still have untouched art supplies from second grade lying around, and stick figures are about all you're capable of (forget trying to draw anything more complicated, like hands . . . *or humans*). But are you *really* a terrible artist? Or is that just a story you've told yourself for years? Just because you weren't a little Picasso at age seven doesn't mean you can't develop some artistic talent at seventeen. What would it hurt if you looked up drawing tutorials on YouTube and gave it a shot?

Or, even if you don't think of yourself as a techie, maybe it's time to learn a little about coding or scripting. Coding, by the way, isn't just for people who want to build computer programs, nor is it just for nerds (such as myself) who are deeply obsessed with technology in all its forms. Learning to code, rather, is pretty much like learning a cheat code for the entire Internet. There are lots of tools and tricks you can use to help you in everyday online situations, like selecting a font that isn't available in your email's WYSIWYG editor (that's short for "What You See Is What You Get"), or discovering an old password that, although you forgot it, is still saved deep inside your computer. Maybe with a little practice, you'll discover an affinity for coding. Or maybe you won't—and that's okay, too.

Why am I asking you to try something you already know you're not interested in? Because it'll open up a whole new part of your brain, that's why! You can't really know for sure what you'll connect with or what you'll be motivated by until you try something. So, try this: pick one skill—drawing, coding, singing, bird-watching, sewing, reading about historical events, whatever—and devote a week to it. For a set period of time every day of that week, commit yourself to learning something about that skill. You've never been into exercising? Try going for a jog, just for five minutes, simply to see how it feels. The next day, do it again. And then do it again the day after that. You hate getting your hands dirty? Try attending a pottery workshop. If you always sign up for chorus, why not dip your toe into acting? If you love writing code, why not try writing a poem? The key is to bust out of your comfort zone. If you try something and you still hate it, well, no harm, no foul. But what if you *don't*? What new and amazing opportunities might present themselves if you suddenly discovered a new talent, a new skill, a new love?

CREATING A CONCEPT VAULT

As you begin exercising your creative muscles and indulging your innate curiosity, you may find yourself inching closer and closer to coming up with that Big Idea. Mine was to start a business, but yours might be to found a club at your school or place of worship, or to gain support for an issue or a movement in your community. Or, you might have lots of little ideas (which can be just as powerful and meaningful as the "big ones"), but you aren't sure which to pursue—or how, or when.

One way to keep those creative impulses coming, without getting overwhelmed or sidetracked or flummoxed (especially if you're a Flip-Flopper), is to write all of those ideas down. Even the crazy ones. Even the what-if-dinosaurs-had-dinosaur-sized-sunglasses type of ideas, which I call "one a.m. thoughts." (You never know, maybe your dinosaur-sized-sunglasses idea will drive you to create a new kind of protective eyewear or something.)

Some of the best ideas I've had concerning my business have leapt from the pages of my Idea Book. For instance, whenever inspiration hits and I get an idea for a clothing or headband design, I sketch it out quickly and jot down the name; then I know I'll be able to create it later, when the time is right. Granted, keeping an Idea Book is a little different from starting a dream board— think of it as a bank where you can save your best ideas for later use—but here are some tips to help get you started.

MAKE YOUR OWN IDEA BOOK

What you'll need: A spiral notebook, diary, journal, or three-ring binder; something to write with; and some discipline.

Write It Down. Whenever a burst of creativity hits you, jot down a short entry with the general idea, write up a super-detailed description complete with concept art and thesis, or do a quick doodle and record a few key words—whatever it takes to get it out of your head and on paper.

Go Old School. Yes, paper. Sure, you could type it up with an app, but I think the things we put on our phones or save online often stay in the digital world, a place where ideas are—in my opinion—easily forgotten. Being able to actually touch the pages and feel the indentations of the words you've written or the pictures you've drawn, on the other hand, brings your ideas into the real world, the place where ideas and concepts can blossom into actions.

Choose the Right Tools. Your Idea Book can be a fancy-looking journal or a cheap spiral sketchbook. It could be a loose-leaf binder that you're constantly adding pages to, or a pocket-sized notebook you tuck in your jacket. You can decorate the cover, or leave it pristine and untouched. It doesn't matter. As long as it has paper, it's an official Idea Book.

Find a Rhythm. There's no hard-and-fast rule concerning how often you should log your ideas—it's not like inspiration strikes every day at the same time (and if it does, I want to meet you!). Just make an effort to find a practice that works for you. With an Idea Book on your desk, atop your nightstand, in your backpack, or wherever, you'll have a physical reminder to do just that.

Keep It Fun, But Take It Seriously. Pay attention to your ideas, even the ones that seem ridiculous. It could be that your "silly" idea for how to conserve water or stop a bully in his tracks is the start of a major project or business or solution.

I believe that all people have been blessed with their own power, their own place, and their own way to influence people around the world, and by now, I hope you're feeling a little more in tune with your passions, your goals, and the things that make you tick. In part II, we'll talk a bit more about how to turn those passions into actions. But for now:

Be creative. Be curious. And watch as your awesomeness is unleashed.

·PART TWO·

Find Your

Path

$\mathcal{E}$arlier in this book, I told you that in the years prior to launching my business, I hadn't even known that it was possible to sell stuff online—I thought that you needed a physical store, and that if *I* ever wanted to sell anything, I'd probably have to buy a building or hire a construction crew (both equally unlikely for an eight-year-old). What I didn't tell you was that I also thought you had to be a grown-up to own a company.

It's not that I thought kids were too immature or too little, per se, I just thought you *had* to be a grown-up. I thought those were the rules. After all, I'd never seen or heard about any other kid entrepreneurs. Had there been a special on Playhouse Disney about kids in business (rather than, or in addition to, the one I'd seen on professional animators), I probably would've jumped right in. But there wasn't at the time, so I figured it just wasn't possible. I thought that no kid would be allowed to open a nonprofit, or head an animation studio, or run a fashion company. I thought being a kid and owning a business might actually be *illegal*.

Obviously, I was wrong about that.

In fact, it wasn't even all that difficult to convince my parents to let me start Maya's Ideas. (As it turns out, running a business is a great way to learn about everything from marketing to money management to math skills—which you'll need in order to purchase supplies, keep your costs in check, and track your revenue.) So the next step in my journey, after getting my parents on board, was setting up my online shop. I read through some FAQs and tutorials on Etsy (incidentally, the site kind of walks you through how to set everything up), then I made an account, created my "store," jumped right in, and got started.

The very first item I uploaded for sale on my shop also happened to be one of the very first headbands I ever created. Instead of a blue ribbon with a yellow flower appliqué, or an orange ribbon with an orange-and-blue flower, this one featured a zebra-print ribbon onto which I sewed a little red butterfly. In addition to being the first item I uploaded, though, "Zebrafly" (the official name I'd given to this particular design) also ended up being the very first item I *sold*. I just hadn't realized that my first sale would happen so quickly.

When I first started designing, photographing, and uploading items to my digital store, I certainly did so with the intention of *selling* them—I mean, why else would anyone spend time on an e-commerce site? But at the same time, I don't think I actually believed that anyone would buy any of the things I had made. It had been only a matter of months since I'd learned it was even possible to sell stuff online; the whole concept was still pretty foreign. So when that first order came through—within days of launching my business—I was pretty much blown away. Someone had actually taken the time to browse the items in my shop, say to herself, *Well, this looks cute*, and then buy something! With her hard-earned money! How crazy is that?!

Since it was my very first order, I knew I couldn't possibly just box up the headband, toss in an invoice, and have that be it—receiving my first order felt celebratory, and I wanted the customer to feel like she was celebrating, too. I wanted to make the package itself seem special.

So I decorated the box with ribbon and plastered stickers all over it. I also dropped in a handwritten thank-you note. (Decorating packages and handwriting thank-you notes is still something I do to this day. I like all the boxes from Maya's Ideas, when they arrive at a customer's doorstep, to make a kind of *grand entrance*.) I can't remember if I went with my dad to the post office to drop off the package—I have a vague memory of waving good-bye to the box before walking out the front door, so it's possible that he dropped it off at the USPS for me. And a few days later, I received my first bit of positive feedback, in the form of a five-star review.

Who knew that my next major milestone would be filling an international order?

Sure, Etsy is a global website, so it's conceivable that a vendor could receive orders from people all over the world. I just hadn't expected *my* third or fourth order—ever—to come from someone in Italy. Immediately, I became consumed with making sure the package would make it to its round-the-world destination. I peppered my parents with questions: *How long would it take to get there? Would we have to buy some kind of special stamps? Did I have to address the package in Italian?!* Thankfully, they kind of took care of the international shipping part for me, which was good: the headband arrived safely, and I wound up with another satisfied customer.

Orders weren't exactly flying in after that—business was pretty slow over the course of those first few months—but whenever I did sell an item, I immediately sat down to conceive and create a new one. That's partly because it hadn't occurred to me that I could create multiples of any one item, and it definitely hadn't occurred to me that more than one person might be interested in purchasing the same thing. (I didn't even realize that I could make multiples without hiring a whole bunch of help. I figured I'd have to design something and then hand the pattern over to a big fancy factory for them to crank out!) On top of that, I didn't have much extra material. It's not like I had yards of zebra-print ribbon lying around; I probably only ever had a couple of butterfly or flower appliqués at a time. When I sold Zebrafly, I certainly didn't have ten more like it just sitting in inventory. So any time an item sold, I'd sit down to think of a totally new design.

Slowly, I started to branch out. My headbands evolved from all-ribbon versions (meant to be tied at the back of your head) to headbands made on a harder, less flexible band. I started working with a wider variety of materials, searching out new types of accents and appliqués to use. Eventually, I moved beyond headbands and began making all types of items: hats, then scarves, and before long, bags and blouses. Whatever popped into my head, I made.

And things continued like that for a while. Over the course of the next year or so, I treated my business more like a hobby, and I mostly made items to sell in my spare time. Sure, I was making money—just not very much. (We're talking twenty dollars here, thirty dollars there. It's not like I was going to be retiring anytime soon.) And, sure, the orders were coming in—but they were spotty. I'd get an order about as often as a tumbleweed rolls through a deserted town in the Old West. Which is to say, not all that often.

Somewhere around the time I turned ten, though, everything changed.

When I first created my Etsy store, I didn't disclose very much about myself, including my age. I'm not sure if that was due to some concern for my privacy or safety, or if it just hadn't occurred to me that my very young age—eight—could be any kind of a selling point. (In fact, I might have considered my age a hindrance. Who knew if people would be more or less inclined to purchase my headbands if they knew I was only eight years old?) As I gained confidence and experience, however, I suddenly felt like revealing a bit more about myself on my seller's page. Since Etsy didn't have a place to include your professional bio back then, I just updated the description of my online store to include some personal information. I mean, I thought what I was doing was pretty cool. Maybe other people would think it was cool, too. So I outed myself as a ten-year-old entrepreneur.

Nowadays, I'm aware that this sort of thing would be deemed self-promotion, but back when I was ten, I knew absolutely nothing about that. I knew nothing about advertising (how would I ever afford that anyway?), and I had no idea that you could drum up publicity via social media. I don't even think I *had* any social media accounts! Anyone who wound up browsing the items available at Maya's Ideas, then, arrived there purely by chance. With a little luck, a potential customer might occasionally discover my Etsy page. So had revealing my age been the only thing that happened, perhaps my business would've never taken off (or perhaps it would have taken longer to take off than it did). But it just so happens that I was on the verge of another development, too.

You see, my mom and I had both become fans of a blog called *Gotham Gal*, written by a New York–based businesswoman named Joanne Wilson. Joanne writes about everything from current events to nonprofit organizations to music and theater, and every Monday she profiles a female entrepreneur. The column is called—wait for it—Women Entrepreneur Mondays. Each and every week, I would read about these amazing and powerful women making their way in the business world, and I was fascinated. Until one day I realized that I was sort of like the women I had been reading about. Of course, at ten I didn't necessarily qualify as a *woman* quite yet, but I decided to email Joanne anyway. I wanted to tell her just how much I loved Women Entrepreneur Mondays and to say how awesome it would be if *I* could be featured. To my delight, Joanne agreed. We arranged a Skype interview, which ended up covering all sorts of random topics, from my company and how I got started, to my favorite Pixar movies, to Taylor Swift, to how much I loved my mom's egg salad sandwiches. (None of those things have changed, by the way. I still love Taylor Swift, and my mom's egg salad sandwiches are still amazing. In fact, I'd like an egg salad sandwich right now. Hold on . . .

. . . and we don't have the ingredients at the moment. Shoot.)

Anyway, Joanne ran the piece, and to this day it remains one of my favorites. That's right—*one* of my favorites. Because, as it turns out, there would be many more articles to come.

One of those was a write-up on the official Etsy blog, written by a woman named Vanessa Bertozzi. We met when she was serving on a panel at the Atlanta campus of Savannah College of Art and Design, and after talking, she said she wanted to feature me! That article actually gave me a chance to debut my first digital animation. (That would be *Ninja Kooky*, which I uploaded to YouTube so the Etsy reporter could embed the video in the post she'd written about me. Who knew that by promoting my business, I'd get a chance to debut my animation projects, too?) Not too much later, I got an email—actually, it was an Etsy direct message—from a reporter at *Forbes* magazine.

I'd heard of *Forbes*—it's a pretty major business publication, if you're wondering—but I didn't know all that much about it. Truthfully, the only magazine I was really familiar with at the time was *National Geographic Kids*. As with any interview request, I discussed this one with my parents, and we decided the piece might be a great way to get the word out about my company and me. The finished product wasn't anything major, just a super-short write-up about a number of "grade school entre-preneurs," but it's the *Forbes* article that I generally credit for helping me make my mark, the one that ulti-mately changed my life.

Because after that, the floodgates opened.

Suddenly, I was fielding requests from Fox 5 Atlanta, a local news channel, and the *Atlanta Journal-Constitution*, my hometown newspaper. With each new article or press appearance, the traffic to my website would go crazy, then die back down a little, then go nuts again. Each time, the ripple effect grew wider. Before I knew it, I was being in-vited to make *national* television appearances, first on the *Steve Harvey* show, which tapes in Chicago—it was my first ride in an airplane!

Now I have an urge to tell you all about that plane trip. Gather around, children, it's story time. So there I was, awoken by my phone alarm at five a.m. I did a weird scramble-type thing out of my butterfly-print bedsheets that I had been under peacefully in an origami fold for about seven hours. I washed up and my mom made me wear a bundle in three layers or so (keep in mind the chill of winter had overstayed its welcome, plus we had to wake up before the sun). From there, I fell asleep in the car to prepare for a grueling three hours of sleeping on the plane. My parents and I arrived at the airport and after going through all of the necessary procedures I went to get a croissant, of course. At that point, the main things that were on my mind were food and wondering how much farther I would have to carry my purple suitcase. There was a smaller bag looped around the handle that occasionally swung from side to side, making it a little bit of a balancing act.

Later, after we'd boarded the plane, I went over ideas about how the ride would feel. Maybe like a spaceship? I was a little bit nervous but mostly excited. Just then, the engines roared to life. I checked to make sure that my seat belt was tight and I braced myself just in case the plane was going to take off like a slingshot or something. Even though I knew that wasn't the case, you can never be too sure.

By the time we were up in the air, I looked out the window as my currently rainy city of Atlanta ever so slowly shrunk. Huge buildings looked like a top view of the peas and carrots that I used to eat when I was five. Roads became just abstract yet organized crisscrosses, and then they all vanished beneath the beautiful and somewhat interrupting clouds.

In between fiddling around with the apps on my iPad, I would glance out the window and kind of space out. Honestly, if you look past the engineering side, planes are so weird. They pretty much are giant tin cans. Sure, it accelerates, but then by some magic force it ascends into the sky. For fun I like to think that a bunch of pegasi help carry the plane all the way to its destination and back, and that the pilot's controls are actually reins to guide them on their way. They don't get tired easily, because they are magic, okay? For Pete's sake, we're talking about horses with wings. Then again, you need a lot of pegasi. Maybe just a giant bird? Or maybe a dragon! Even cooler. A friendly dragon, though. Friendly dragons are super-cool.

Moving on, soon after I made my appearance on *Steve Harvey*, I made an appearance on the ABC morning show *The View*.

I've been watching *The View* since I was little (and by "watching," I really mean playing on the floor of the living room while my mom watched), so to get an email from one of the producers inviting me to appear on an episode about "cool kids" was surreal. Within a matter of days, I was on a plane to New York, arriving at the ABC soundstage, and shaking hands with the amazing and awesome Whoopi Goldberg. (She was very gracious and down-to-earth—I just loved her!) Of course, all this attention for my business was not *just* a lot of fun, it also resulted in a lot of sales. I was able to hire a few full-time employees, as well as start a college fund. In the space of just a few short years, Maya's Ideas had grown beyond even my wildest dreams.

The success of my company, however, has been about so much more than getting press or selling stuff. It's opened up doors for me to meet various inspiring and influential people who have become not just my heroes, but also my friends. For example, I met Eve Ensler, the wonderful author, playwright, and women and girls' rights activist (best known for writing *The Vagina Monologues*), at an event in Atlanta for her book *In the Body of the World*. I instantly felt like we were kindred spirits. You could see the rainbow of her aura. The energy I got from her was warm and electric. I've never seen or felt anything like it on anyone I've met before, and it was only strengthened when she gave me a big bear hug shortly after I introduced myself. Meeting her was like reuniting with an old friend. Since then, she's become a big supporter of mine. It was at Eve's event that I met the great Pat Mitchell, the CEO of the Paley Center for Media and the former president and CEO of PBS, as well as the founder of the TED-Women events. The work she has done to empower and inspire women—including me!—is truly amazing. Pat is actually the one who invited me to speak on the global TED stage. I met the wonderful Laura Turner Seydel a few years ago, at an Eco-Fashion and Accessories Trunk Show she happened to be attending in my hometown. Laura is chairperson of the Captain Planet Foundation, an organization that supports environmental stewardship by awarding grants to youth-driven projects. She travels all over the world encouraging youth to be environmentally conscious, and I'm super-proud to have donated to her organization. I've also met the amazing Dr. Bernice King, daughter of Dr. Martin Luther King Jr.; she and I met at the King Center's annual Salute to Greatness Awards dinner. Later, she invited me to speak at an event to commemorate the fiftieth anniversary of her father being awarded the Nobel Peace Prize. I can feel her strength in her presence; it touches and inspires everyone who meets her. Each of these relationships led to another introduction; each opportunity led to another open door.

And that's what happens when you trust yourself enough to follow your instincts and your passions: you'll find new possibilities that you probably never imagined opening up to you. My passions certainly took me in a new direction. Partly based on those relationships, I've been able to launch a thriving career as a public speaker. I never thought I'd have the chance to stand in front of groups of people all over the United States and the world to talk about myself and my ideas. (And I *really* never imagined that I'd love doing it!) I've also had ample opportunity to give back—through environmental activism, outreach, and donations to nonprofit organizations and charities (but we'll talk more about that in part III). In ways I couldn't have imagined when I was first starting out, my business has had deeply personal significance, too.

My grandmother Marguerite was the centerpiece of my family. She was a strong, amazing, independent woman (she had to raise seven kids all on her own after my grandfather passed, back when my mom was just three). My parents and I used to love making surprise visits to Charlotte, North Carolina, to see her. She used to tell me that I was "all sweetness and goodness." I remember sitting in her chair by the china cabinet, talking to her while admiring all her beautiful glass figurines.

She passed away in 2013, and in her memory I designed an item of clothing called Marguerite's Garden. Anyone who knew her knew that she loved her flowers, so the design, a sort of scarf meets necklace, features lots of crocheted flowers and leaves. I wore it during my TEDWomen talk to give me strength. All of the proceeds from the sale of the item go to women's organizations, which I know would have made her proud. I feel like Marguerite's Garden is a garden in heaven, flourishing with everlasting love for her children, grandchildren, and great-grandchildren. Dewdrops reflecting her strength, birds singing songs of her kindness, the sun's rays shining on her legacy. Her garden is full of beauty and life. To have created something in her honor, something that could actually affect the lives of others in a positive way, is one of the most important and profound experiences I've ever had.

Ryan Lash / TED

These days, I'm working to take Maya's Ideas to the next level. I've been approached by several retailers (including some local boutiques and a national chain) that are interested in carrying my designs—and while those deals are still very much works in progress, they mean I'm one step closer to eventually selling my creations in an actual brick-and-mortar store (no building-buying or construction crew required!). I've already brought in some outside help in the form of full-time employees; slowly, I'm building up my inventory, and I'm preparing to scale up the company to deal with increased demand.

I still sometimes have to pinch myself when I think of all that's happened in the last seven years. There's no way

I could ever have predicted that the business I started as an eight-year-old would propel me to the national, even global stage—and before my sixteenth birthday, no less. And while there are no guarantees in life, if you're looking for a secret to my success, it would be this: My creativity and curiosity started me down a path. I chose to follow it.

Who knows where *your* path might lead?

SO YOU'VE GOT AN IDEA . . . NOW WHAT?

Maya's Ideas came about when, after receiving compliments on my homemade headbands and discovering the website Etsy, I was suddenly struck with that Big Idea. If you follow *your* creativity and curiosity, you'll undoubtedly be struck with a Big Idea, too (or maybe you'll have lots of little ideas—don't discount those; I was serious when I said they could be just as influential and meaningful as the big ones). But what comes *after* that Big Idea? What are the next steps you should take? How do you really get started?

Prospective business owners, in the earliest stages of launching their companies, usually put together something called a "business plan"—basically just a written report that outlines the company's goals, and provides a kind of road map for achieving those goals. A typical business plan might include a market analysis (a way to identify potential customers), a sales strategy (a plan to reach those customers), financial projections (how much revenue the company should make), and management structure (a breakdown of who's in charge). The simple act of writing a business plan can help a wannabe entrepreneur learn more about the company she intends to build.

Similarly, you'll want to come up with a plan, too. Think of it as your Big Idea Strategy. True, you probably won't need to prepare a market analysis (especially if your Big Idea has nothing to do with business), but it's always a good idea to have a clear sense of what you want to achieve. Here are some tips to help you get started:

Arm Yourself with Information

It's true that launching my business didn't exactly require months of planning—the Etsy site itself features lots of tutorials and tips to help potential sellers open their stores. Even after reading through all those articles, though, there were still some things I needed to figure out before I could really get started. One of those things was pricing. Since I was only eight, I had no real concept of how much (or how little) my items should cost. It's not like I had a checking account, and the only time I ever bought anything was with my mom. (Either I'd pick something out for *her* to purchase, or walk up to the counter and buy something with *her* money.) In order to determine the right price point for my items, then, I had to do some research. First, I needed to factor in the cost of my materials (for example, if the ribbons and appliqués I needed cost $5, but I sold each finished headband for only $4, I'd quickly go broke). I also poked around other Etsy stores and e-commerce sites to get a sense of what other vendors were charging.

There's an old saying that applies to anyone who's trying to do something he or she has never done before: you don't know what you don't know. So the first thing you'll need when you get ready to launch your Big Idea is information. For example, if you're interested in starting an official club at your school, you'll need to figure out what, if any, rules you must follow. Must you host a certain number of meetings? Boast a certain number of members? Do you need sponsorship from a teacher or guidance counselor? Where will you hold your meetings, and will you need permission to use the facilities during after-school hours? To find the answers to those questions, you might want to swing by the administration office to ask about paperwork and protocol. You might want to speak with the heads of other on-campus clubs, too. Ask about their experiences. What worked for them? What might they have done differently if they could start over?

Or, like me, let's say you have an interest in animation. In addition to teaching yourself about different styles and techniques (I mentioned already that watching behind-the-scenes footage of my favorite movies was a great place to get started), you might want to learn more about the profession itself (animators work primarily in film and television, but also in advertising and the computer and digital industries—think video games and iPhone apps), as well as the process (long before an animator begins his work, he'll likely have seen—or even helped create—storyboards and 2-D or 3-D models). Whatever you're into, arming yourself with information is the first step toward realizing that Big Idea.

Outline Your Goals

What's the intention behind the launch of your Big Idea?
Are you starting a club with the hope of making an environmental impact? Want to help people around the world
have access to clean drinking water? Trying to outlaw bullying behaviors from your school? Are you hoping to mon-
etize your idea for the purpose of making a profit? It
doesn't really matter what your goals are, but taking the
time to think about them—and to write them down!—can
help ensure that you stay on target.

Carve Out the Time

Everyone knows that you can't expect great results if you
don't put in the work, but carving out time to follow your
passions is sometimes easier said than done, especially if
you already have a jam-packed schedule. After all, pursuing that Big Idea might mean less time for goofing
around online, shopping, Skyping, or gaming; it might

even mean skipping the occasional get-together with friends (at least in the beginning stages, when you're trying to get your project off the ground). One trick I've learned is to schedule time to work on my passion projects right into my days and weeks, the same way I'd schedule time for school and homework, church on Sundays, dinner with my family in the evenings, and the occasional sleepover. I find that when I *don't* set aside that time on my schedule—when I just try to fit it in—it's too easy to let days, weeks, and even months slip by without progress.

Own Your Idea(s)

I mentioned that my original Etsy page didn't divulge very much personal information about myself, including my age. But in the early days of my company, I also failed to give myself a title, like "CEO" or "creator" or "owner." (Granted, I don't think I actually knew what a CEO was when I was eight, and anyway, I thought of myself more as an artist or designer.) After I started getting some press attention, though, I realized that writers and reporters were starting to call me a "CEO" or an "entrepreneur." It was only *after* people started using those labels that I began to feel comfortable with the terms. So sometime around age twelve—four long years after launching Maya's Ideas—I finally gave myself the title I'd always deserved.

Don't make the same mistake that I did.

Sometimes people, especially kids, can be hesitant to call themselves CEOs or entrepreneurs because it can seem kind of boastful. But it's important to give yourself credit when it's deserved. Sure, if you haven't so much as sold a garment yet, you might hold off on calling yourself a professional fashion designer. And there's no need to *inflate* your title (if what you're really doing is babysitting on the occasional weeknight, there's no need to call yourself an Executive Child Rearing and Baby Care Commander in Chief). If you do recognize yourself as a CEO (or an artist/activist/philanthropist/designer/coder), though, others will be more likely to recognize you as that thing, too. Owning your ideas, your contributions, and your accomplishments is an important step toward being taken seriously.

Do What You Love

I often say that starting a business can be both a blessing and a curse—but that applies to pursuing just about any creative idea. On the one hand, a successfully implemented Big Idea can produce opportunities you haven't even dreamed of. After all, I certainly never expected to be a role model or become a public speaker; those were unexpected opportunities that presented themselves as I followed my path. On the other hand, Big Ideas come with Big Responsibilities. (No one else is going to run my business but me—that job is all on my shoulders.) But the thing that keeps me going, even when things get a little bit tough, is simple: working on my company doesn't feel like *work*. Primarily, it's fun. I get to exercise my creative mind by coming up with new items to sell, and I'm constantly learning new things that I can use in everyday life.

I like to think of Big Ideas as being a little like babies or children: It's up to you to either nurture your ideas to help them grow, or to abandon them. It's up to you to help your idea through the occasional stumbles and roadblocks until it's one day able to walk on its own. This is why it's vital to do something you enjoy, that you don't view your Big Idea as a burden or a hardship. Because if you truly love whatever magical idea your brain gives birth to, you'll be that much more likely to ensure that it blossoms.

BUILDING A SUPPORT NETWORK

Recruiting Traveling Companions on Your Creative Journey

As you begin following a path toward realizing that Big Idea, you'll quickly discover that you need a support network in place, because none of us can accomplish anything entirely alone. Well, I mean, sure, we can all do *some* things alone. You probably don't need help brushing your teeth or doing your math homework. (Scratch that: you probably don't need help *brushing your teeth*—I totally need help with my math homework sometimes.) But when it comes to pursuing your creative passions, you're definitely going to need some help. That help might come in the form of emotional support (encour-

---

You Got This!

agement when you feel down, bored, or distracted, someone to cheer you up whenever you hit one of life's speed bumps); practical or logistical support (someone to help you edit your film, organize a protest rally, or post flyers all over your hometown); or even financial assistance (someone to help you raise money or launch a crowdfunding campaign). And even if you manage to get through those initial steps alone, you're still going to need support later—even the kind you never actually asked for. Think about it: if you want to be a filmmaker, people are going to have to watch (and like!) your films. Ditto for a fashion designer (you'll need customers to willingly purchase your clothes). Or an activist (you'll need people to join your movement). Whatever you want to accomplish, you're going to need as much support as possible to get your ideas out into the world. That's what this section is about: building a team of traveling companions to help you on your creative journey. And for that first component of your support network, you won't have to look very far.

After all, you're gonna need their permission . . .

Getting Your Parents On Board

Ah, parents (or grandparents or guardians—whoever's in charge of raising *you*). They basically have one job, which is to make sure you can survive in the world without destroying it—or yourself. Of course, they'll probably want to ensure that you have lots of fun, lots of love, and a bright future, too. But as we all know, when it comes to getting their permission to do, well, *anything*, it's necessary to create an airtight argument, a top-notch pitch. It's almost like going on *Shark Tank*, but instead of trying to get capital for your business, you're trying to negotiate a boost to your allowance or a trip to the mall. In fact, you may find yourself plotting and planning for weeks—*How am I gonna convince them to let me go to that party?*—even about the not-so-important stuff. Which is why, when it comes to the super-duper-important stuff, like permission or support to follow your passion, you have to work even harder. A lot harder than you'd have to work to, say, convince your mom to let you eat that leftover pasta that was meant for your dad . . . even though you really like pasta . . . and you're really hungry . . . and you doubt he'd even notice if you ate it anyway . . . (Yes, this totally happened to me recently. Outcome: I ate the pasta. And it was great.)

I had to pitch my parents when I wanted to start my business, but as I told you previously, they were almost immediately and totally on board (much to my delight and surprise). Since not everything is quite that simple, I've got some tips to help you explain your Big Idea to your folks. Every parent has a different style, a different way of communicating and offering support, but generally speaking, I think you can break them down into three different types:

✴ The Up-for-Anything Parents

Up-for-Anything Parents do whatever they can to make your creative dreams a reality—they drive you to the art supply store and give you money for materials, enroll you in that dance class (then let you drop ballet and take modern jazz), help you post flyers/create a website/organize a rally for the cause you're passionate about. They give you room to grow, and offer the occasional bit of constructive criticism. They build you up and respect your opinions. One or both of your parents may even share your creative passion—perhaps you inherited it from them.

Now, just because you have Up-for-Anything Parents doesn't mean they'll let you do whatever you want. You'll still need to explain your Big Idea, as well as the reasons why you want to pursue it. The first step to getting them on board—for these and for all other types of parents— is to communicate. I know it may be natural to ramble on and explain things awkwardly, since that's sometimes how we talk to our folks on a daily basis, but you want to be clear. And you want to be serious. If you have any articles, videos, or examples of other successful people in your field (and you should, if you've been working on that Big Idea Strategy), now's the time to trot those out. If you've done actual work in the area you want to pursue—a song you wrote, an animation you created, a report you aced—now's the time to show them. These examples and exhibits will not only help you explain your idea, they'll also help demonstrate your passion and commitment to it.

If you're wondering whether a formal sit-down with your parents is really necessary, or if you can bring up your

Big Idea in a more casual way, that's really up to you. But certainly you probably don't need to stage a full-scale family meeting. There's no need to create a PowerPoint presentation. Just focus on stating your goals, presenting some basic facts and research, and describing the positive impact of your Big Idea (to you, to your community, to the whole world—whatever).

✳ The Follow-in-My-Footsteps Folks

The Follow-in-My-Footsteps types of parents are often extremely creative and passionate people, but they want you to grow up and do the same things that *they* do. Maybe you come from a family of musicians, for example, but your heart is set on coding and web design. Or maybe you come from a long line of medical doctors, but you see yourself acting on the big screen. It's a common situation, but it's also a tough one. There's just not much worse than being forced to drink something that isn't your cup of tea.

First things first: remind yourself that music and web design, for example, are vastly different fields (as are acting and medicine). The knowledge that you want to pursue something much, much different than your parents, then, could come as a bit of a shock. And, really, can you blame them?

Next, consider that the parent who wants you to follow in his or her footsteps probably has a clear idea of what doing so would help you achieve. For example, maybe your dad wants you to become a doctor because it's a prestigious career with a large salary, and he never wants to see you struggle. Or, perhaps your painter mother and your poet dad think you should pursue a career in the arts because they want you to have a career that you're passionate about (rather than a "boring" nine-to-five office job). Stop and ask yourself, *Will my passion help me achieve that thing my parents want for me?* If the answer is yes, tell them about it. For example: "Mom, I know you want me to become a pianist because you love playing so much, but that's exactly how I feel about coding and web design."

※ The Parent Who Just Doesn't Get It
    (Your Passion, That Is)

You may communicate often and have a perfectly healthy relationship, but you and your parents seem to be on two totally different planets most of the time. It's not that the Parent Who Just Doesn't Get It isn't supportive, it's just that what you're trying to accomplish may seem wacky, weird, or totally foreign to him or her. Parents like these are also often more practical than passionate. For example, they may be much more concerned about your grades than enrolling you in a dance class or sports club.

Ask yourself: Is it possible that they're a little bit right? *Do* you need to focus for a time on getting your grades up? Is it possible you can come to some kind of compromise?

It's conceivable that no amount of (polite, respectful) communication will change your parent's mind. If that's the case, you may have to put your passion on hold until a time when you *are* free to pursue it. Don't, however, just sit around doing nothing. Search out other projects you might want to pursue in the meantime. And don't worry if this new passion has nothing to do with your old one—expanding creatively has never been a bad thing!

Growing Your Circle of Friends

Although it's true that you generally don't have to *pitch* your friends to get them on board with your Big Idea, friends are still a hugely important and influential part of your support network. (After all, who else can you complain about your parents to?) It's also true that friends come in all shapes and sizes, and will fulfill all different sorts of roles in your life.

For example, there's the friend you turn to for advice, the often older, wiser kid who seems to have it all figured out. There's the friend you call when you need to dump your emotions or hash things out, what I like to call a

"venting buddy," someone you can wallow in angst with once in a while. There's the friend you share interests with—maybe that's your "karate friend." You study at the same dojo, but you really don't see him or her more than once or twice a week. The long-term friend, who's been around since you were in diapers, who's more like a sister or a brother at this point. The fun-to-goof-off-with friend, who's always good for a chuckle. And the super-duper best friend, the person who you just can't imagine living your life without. Aside from all the laughing, venting, karate, late-night talks, and last-minute homework help, though, friends can be amazingly supportive on your creativity journey, too.

Anna Rose and Sarah Jane happen to be two of my closest friends. They're both artists, musicians, and all-around creative people (not to mention sisters, too!). We love to paint and draw together; sometimes we even do improv comedy work. One of the best parts of our friendship, though, is the way we build each other up and support each other's Big Ideas: Anna Rose and Sarah Jane are always quick to say congratulations when something great happens, always ready with a high five or a social media shout-out or retweet. Meanwhile, I'm always there to root for and cheer on their endeavors. Watching them embark on their own passion projects inspires me to stay on my path, work harder, and do better, too.

A strong, supportive group of friends will not only look out for you, they'll also challenge you and help you grow as a person. Of course, the whole challenge one another thing doesn't mean your friends are running up to you and screaming, "I dare you to get better at [insert passion here]!" That would be weird, and sort of rude. It just means that your friends are in touch with their own unique creativity and are passionate about their work (which hopefully encourages you to commit to yours), as well as supportive of what you're doing. They're the type of friends who encourage you to enter your films in a local festival or point you in the direction of a cool art college or a seminar you should check out. Friends like these can even become a *part* of your Big Idea, by joining forces with you and collaborating with you to turn your vision into the real thing.

Even if you already have tons of friends, it's never a bad idea to expand your circle, particularly by including people who share your ambition and specific creative interests. After all, friends who are into the same things as you can sometimes help you out in ways that others in your group just aren't capable of. For example, one of my friends recently told me that she, too, was interested in animation, but she had no idea how or where to get started. And it was easy for me to point her in the right direction: I sent her some resources and tutorials to check out. I also recommended to her two different animation software programs (one is admittedly a little pricey, the other is free; I figured she might like to practice on the free one before upgrading to the more advanced version).

New friends who share common interests, by the way, are probably closer than you might think. They could be members of a club that you're interested in joining at school, people you meet at an art fair or in an acting class, or someone you notice hanging out in a Facebook group (because, hey, there's a Facebook group for just about any interest these days). Speaking of Facebook, the Internet is another great place to meet like-minded people.

I met my friend Asch on Tumblr, largely because we

both like geeky stuff like anime and costuming. One day (long after we developed an online friendship), I discovered that we actually live in the same state! We don't live close enough to hang out in person very often, but we do meet up at sci-fi and gaming conventions, like MomoCon and DragonCon. Then we talk online for the rest of the year. (I've also got friends who I originally met IRL but who have since moved into the digital realm—like Victoria, who I met in church not long before she moved with her family to Florida.)

Just because these friends are *online* friends doesn't mean they can't offer just as much support and companionship as your IRL versions. In fact, you can do lots of the same things with your online circle as your IRL friends. I'm constantly playing games, talking on Skype, or watching movies with my online crew (when we're not talking about or working on our Big Ideas, that is!).

A WORD ABOUT INTERNET
SMARTS AND SAFETY

Whenever we got access to our first computer, we almost certainly got a version of the "Internet safety talk": don't reveal your name or your address, or talk to strangers online. Of course, that probably went out the window as soon as you joined Club Penguin. It went even further out the window when digital communication (emails, text messages, online shopping, and networking and gaming) became a part of everyone's daily lives. There are, however, some important things to keep in mind when making friends in the digital world. And here's the most important one of all: Don't be dumb. That's right. Don't do dumb things on the Internet.

It's strange, isn't it? I mean, everyone has been warned about what he or she should and should not do online. Everyone knows there are some comments you shouldn't make, some pictures you shouldn't post, some people you shouldn't communicate with, and some details that you shouldn't reveal about yourself. Everyone has thought, *Oh I would never do* [fill in the blank]. *That's weird* [or gross or crude or just not the right thing to do]. All of us have rolled our eyes when our parents warned us—again—about exercising online smarts. And then so many of us promptly forget everything we know and go right ahead and do that dumb thing anyway, with little to no regard for the consequences. Don't be one of these people. Remember that you cannot simply delete a post or a picture and expect it to be gone. Whatever you do online exists forever, lurking somewhere in the depths of some super-computer. Don't be dumb. Exercising Internet smarts really is that plain and simple.

✴ When Good Friends Drift Apart

One of my first true friends—not merely someone I was made to play with back when we were both in diapers, but someone I really clicked with on a deep, emotional level—was a girl named Beth. (By the way, that's not her real name.) It was springtime, and my mother and I were planting pansies around the mailbox to spiff up the front yard when Beth walked right up and said hello. We hit it off immediately, and went on to have lots of adventures together: We'd swap silly bandz, play with plushies, gorge ourselves on mac and cheese and chicken nuggets. One winter we went sledding through the backyard on inner tubes designed for the pool (which, truthfully, didn't end well). We even had our own show, *The Maya and Beth Show*, which I filmed and edited. We made only one or two episodes, but it was so much fun (even if those episodes were mostly just footage of us running around and screaming).

A year or two later, however, our friendship had started to fizzle. It was summertime then, and Beth was in and out of town constantly, visiting relatives here, taking a family vacation there. Since she wasn't around much, it got harder and harder to stay in touch. And the longer we went without speaking, the easier it was to just let the friendship begin to peter out. It's not like we had a fight or anything; there was no major conflict, there were no hard feelings. On some level, we probably each just got too lazy or distracted to pick things back up again, to reach out and call each other. Instead, we just moved on with our own lives.

When you have a close or even a best friend, someone you're used to talking to multiple times a day, someone with whom you share almost everything, and you suddenly sense some growing distance between you, well, that can feel pretty weird. The reality is that it's normal to grow apart from some of our childhood friends, though. We all change and evolve as we get older—including you. At some point, you and someone you're close to now will likely go your separate ways, even if it seems strange to think about right this moment.

Now, having what I call a yo yo friend is a situation that gets a little more complicated.

I once knew a girl I'll call Julie (not her real name, either), whom I considered for a time to be my very best friend in the whole wide world, and the world is a pretty big place. We talked about good things and bad, enjoyed hanging out, and genuinely supported each other. But for some reason I couldn't understand, our relationship started to change. One day she just completely stopped replying to my texts, calls, and social media messages (even though I could tell she was still reading them). One day we were great, and the next we were not so chill.

Looking back on it now, I think she might have fallen in with a new group of friends—and that part is completely and totally normal. What sucked, however, is that she would communicate with me only when she had something *she* wanted to say. I'd respond, chat back and forth, and be there for her, but as soon as I wanted to talk about something going on in my life, she'd read the message but fail to respond. That same thing kept happening over and over again.

For a long time, I didn't say anything about it. I convinced myself that she was just really busy. (Although, if she *was* really that busy, why would she bother taking the time to read my messages at all?) Or, I thought something might be going on at school or in her personal life. I gently reminded her that whatever the issue was, she could talk to me about it and I would listen. No response. I'd message her and say, "Hey, do you just have a lot going on right now?" Nothing. Then, after months of flat-out ignoring me, she'd get in touch to talk about something she thought was cool. The whole friendship had become totally lopsided. Clearly, we were no longer on the same wavelength.

Eventually, I decided to confront Julie. "Hey, I'm kinda stressed out over here? I don't understand why you won't respond to my texts or calls." (As much as I was stressed out, though, I'm sure that the harder I tried to work things out, the more and more stressed she got, too.) Still nothing. I had so much anxiety built up about the situation—I felt like such a yo-yo, constantly being yanked back and forth—that I finally had to acknowledge that the relationship just wasn't healthy or fun anymore. Although we still speak every once in a while (and only when she initiates it), the genuine friendship we shared has ended. It took some time, but I had to learn to be okay with that.

All friends fight sometimes. If you know that those fights only serve to bring you and your friend closer, then that's okay. But if you have a friendship that results in constant craziness and arguments and stress—especially if the other person isn't doing anything to improve the situation—that's just not good.

So, what's a girl (or a guy) to do? If you realize that one of your friends isn't acting like the person you thought she was, talk to her. Tell her how you're feeling. If you used to value a particular one of her qualities (like her honesty or her work ethic), or if she seems to be making a decision that's in direct opposition to her stated values, you owe it to her (as well as to your friendship) to speak up. There's a reason that the golden rule ("Do unto others as you would have them do unto you") is, well, the golden rule.

Unfortunately, talking to that friend won't always work. It can be sad, even heartbreaking, when one of your super-close friends doesn't appear to care about the relationship anymore. *Whomp-whomp.* You'd also think it would be easy to disassociate yourself from someone when he or she starts acting like a total jerk-face, but it's not. Just remember that any relationship—not only a romantic one—can become unhealthy (or, in extreme cases, even abusive). If you feel trapped, like you can't speak your mind without the other person getting mad, you might want to consider phasing that friendship out. You deserve to get back what you give. Standing up for yourself and insisting on being treated well in your relationships is an important part of growing up.

✳ Standing Out from the Crowd

I've always worn my hair natural—I've never even thought about having it relaxed at any point in my fifteen years on this earth. So one day when I was about eight years old, not long after I'd joined a website where kids could be creative and share stories with each other, I made a short video about my favorite subjects (spelling, Spanish, science, and art), and in it, I had my signature fro going on.

A few days later, I noticed the video had received a smattering of likes and comments, but one girl posted that I "needed a perm." I wasn't particularly offended at the time, mostly because I didn't know what a perm was. Unfortunately, it wouldn't be the only time someone judged me based solely on the way I style my hair.

On a day not long after reading that comment, it snowed in Atlanta, which is an extremely rare, some might even say magical, thing for people who live in the southernmost states. So like virtually every other kid in my neighborhood (and probably the whole metro Atlanta area), I bundled up and headed outside. My hair happened to be braided, and since it was cold, it was tucked up under my hat. After a long day of tossing snowballs and making snow squirrels, I went home, nose runny and hands numb, but happy.

By the next morning, the snow had already begun to melt, so all the kids headed back outside again, determined to enjoy it before it was gone. This time, though, I'd forgone the hat. Once again, my hair was in full-on fro mode. At the time, I thought nothing of this. Long before that perm comment, my mom had instilled in me the idea that my natural hair was beautiful. Sure, it's fluffy and poofy and tangles easily, but I loved it all the same. That is, until my friend and I popped over to her house for a snack. Her brother happened to be there. This was a kid whom I'd spoken to before; we even had a kind of casual friendship. But he took one look at me and a smug sort of smile crept across his face. "What's wrong with your hair?" were the first words out of his mouth.

I think I said something along the lines of "This is how I always wear it," but I was still only eight, and was therefore shocked and a little confused. I didn't quite know what to think or how I should feel. Insulted? Embarrassed? I think what I really felt was disappointed: his words had made me suddenly uncomfortable. I felt a self-consciousness about my hair that had never been there before. (Luckily, I was able to get over that.)

The people around us—our friends, our acquaintances, and our classmates—are absolutely influential in our lives, in both positive and negative ways. They can push us forward and inspire us to reach for our dreams, or they can hold us back. Some kids (and adults) are way too focused on what other people think. They allow themselves to be overly influenced by the media or their peers, and they think it's perfectly normal to pressure others into making those same choices: *You shouldn't wear those clothes, take those classes, or wear your hair like that. You should conform. You should be like everyone else. Don't be different. Don't stick out.*

Look, it's natural to care what others think of you (and it can even be healthy, to a certain extent). But it's sad when you care so much about fitting in that you start to reject the very things that make you unique and special. After all, the greatest inventions and innovations were made by people who *didn't* just do what everyone else was doing. How are you supposed to pursue your passions and chase that Big Idea if all you're interested in is being a part of the crowd? I mean, sure, the crowd is popular, but is that really what matters?

Ask yourself: Does the crowd or group you long to fit in with stand up for what's right? Do they use their voices to inspire and help others? Do they treat everyone as equals, because they know that everyone is unique and awesome in his or her own special way? Are they curious to seek out and learn more about the world around them? To preserve it? To improve it? Does your group fit each (or at least most) of those categories?

Whom you hang out with and aspire to be like will absolutely affect your future, as well as the person you become. So find that special spark within you, and don't be afraid to share it. Show the world that you love yourself, flaws, quirks, poofy hair, and all. Do that, and your true friends will follow.

Finding a Mentor

A few years ago, I decided to launch a crowdfunding campaign in order to round up more capital to grow my business. Since I'd never really done anything like that before, I knew that I'd likely need some guidance and help. So, I reached out to a few prominent businesspeople via email. One of those was Alexis Ohanian, the cofounder of Reddit.

It's true that Alexis was famous for running a tech company, while I was running a clothing business. And I might never have reached out to him if it weren't for his message and his unique experience. He's been an activist and an advocate for an open Internet, a prominent supporter of entrepreneurs (in all fields), and a champion for grassroots crowdfunding platforms like Kickstarter. Alexis and his team offered some great tips and advice for my campaign, and I kept the connection going and the lines of communication open. About a year later, I found out that Alexis would be coming to my hometown as part of a national book tour.

Alexis and I finally got a chance to meet in person more than a year after I sent him that first email, on the day before my fourteenth birthday. Ever since then, he's become an incredible source of guidance, inspiration, and professional support. I can reach out to him when I want or need to discuss a potential business opportunity or would like to ask an entrepreneurial question. Meanwhile, he's given me a couple of very public shout-outs, including talking about me during an appearance on a Chicago-area morning news show, and tweeting about me during his attendance at the South by Southwest music, film, and tech festival. Alexis is awesome, funny, and incredibly business savvy, so I'm honored to have him as a mentor, as well as a friend.

When you're in the early stages of pursuing that Big Idea, mentors can be incredibly important. And I don't mean wise, old, you-have-much-to-learn-young-grasshopper–type mentors (although those aren't bad, either). After all, mentors aren't mystical, magical, all-knowing beings, they're really just people with firsthand experience in the field that you're interested in working in. They can provide advice, suggestions, connections, and—perhaps most important—emotional, financial, and logistical support. It's sometimes suggested that a mentor is so above the mentee that the two can't have an actual friendship or an emotional connection. But I've found that you don't need to be distant from or subservient to or beneath someone to learn important lessons from them. The only important qualification for a successful mentor-mentee relationship, really, is mutual and equal respect. With enough time and a deep enough connection, mentors can very easily (and very often) morph into friends, or what I like to call friend-tors.

I have many different friend-tors who have played many different roles in my journey. For example, I had an opportunity to speak at a women business owner's conference hosted by Womenetics, because I was invited by Bonnie Chapman, a women and girls' rights activist. After our first in-person meeting, Bonnie and I not only developed a friendship, she also helped put me in touch with other women and girls' rights groups, including Girls Inc. I frequently turn to another friend-tor, the amazing, creative, and insightful Allison "Wonders" Gars, a life and speaking coach, for guidance and support when I prepare for big public engagements like my TEDWomen talk. Allison and I met because she often works with speakers at various TEDx events around the country; these days, I call her whenever I'm working on a new talk. Scott Weiss, the CEO of Speakeasy, a communication consulting firm, and his team have also helped me prepare. They are great at helping me make sure I'm getting my message across, that I'm accomplishing all that I want to whenever I'm sharing my personal story with young people and aspiring entrepreneurs. And another friend-tor, Cheryl Burnside, an activist and founder of a women's health nonprofit, gave me my first paid speaking engagement at a girls' empowerment event. Initially, *she* contacted *me*, but over the years, we've strengthened our relationship, and she's become a major supporter of everything I'm doing. Finally, when I was getting one of my nonprofit projects off the ground (we'll talk more about that in part III), I reached out to Derreck Kayongo. Derreck (a 2011 Top 10 CNN Hero) is the founder of the Global Soap Project, a nonprofit that distributes recycled soap to people in developing countries and individuals in need. We had a really cool meeting, after which he took me over to CARE, one of the largest humanitarian organizations in the world, and introduced me to the amazing Dr. Helene Gayle, CARE's then president. These are just some examples of the friend-tors in my life.

As crazy as it seems, I met many of these people the same way I met Alexis of Reddit fame—I just reached out, introduced myself, and asked for advice. You'll probably be amazed at how many people are willing (even eager) to help you, once you ask them for assistance or information. Now, you may be thinking, *Sure, Maya, all that sounds great, but how on earth do I find a mentor?* The first thing you'll need to do is *identify* a potential mentor or two. If you're already familiar with someone who works in the same or a similar field, then great—you can proceed to the next step (which we'll get to in just a bit). But if you have no idea whom to contact, if you can't think of a single person who might have some advice or wisdom to share, then you'll have to do some research.

You can start with a simple Google search, like "fashion designers on Twitter" or "female entrepreneurs in [insert your hometown]." Remember that a mentor doesn't have to be famous or even particularly well known—it could be a guy who went to your high school who's now an activist at his local college; it could be the owner of a nearby dance studio/bookstore/clothing boutique; it could even be your local congressperson. Keep in mind, too, that it's a good idea to seek out mentors who *don't* work in your desired field—it really doesn't matter if you want to open a bakery, focus on web development, or run a video game company; in the end, it's all business. What matters most is that your mentor genuinely cares about your goals, ideas, and views.

Once you've identified a potential mentor, it's time to reach out. If they have contact information listed on their website, feel free to email. A Facebook message or LinkedIn invite can work, too. Even a direct (read: private) message on Twitter can get the ball rolling. And remember, just because you've identified one mentor doesn't mean that you won't find another. You'll encounter many amazing people as you continue following your path. So you never know where (or when) you and your next potential mentor might meet!

EMAILING A PROSPECTIVE MENTOR

You may feel a little nervous reaching out to a mentor, especially if the person you have in mind is very well known, but try not to worry about that. If this person is truly willing to help or guide you, he or she will. And if not, that's okay, too. There are a lot of fish (mentors) in the sea (business world), so to speak. Here's how to make your business email, private Facebook note, or direct Twitter message more likely to snag one.

Step 1: Introduce yourself. I know, I know. This sounds pretty basic. And yet I've received countless emails where the sender jumps right into the heart of the message, while I'm left sitting there thinking, *Um, who are you?* Your introduction doesn't have to be overly formal or fancy; it could be as simple as "Hi, I'm such-and-such, the founder of so-and-so." Or, if you haven't actually founded anything, you could try this: "I'm such-and-such and I'm passionate about [fill in the blank]."

Furthermore, a good introduction helps explain how you discovered the person to whom you're writing (although this might not be necessary if the person you're reaching out to is famous, a celebrity, or a household name). A simple "I read an article about you in [insert publication here]" can go a long way. Be sure to tell prospective mentors that you love or admire or respect the work they're doing, or tell them a story about how they helped inspire you. Remember that it can be hard to connect with someone through a wall of text, so do your best to make your personality shine through as much as possible. After all, when we're emotionally connected to someone, we're more likely to be interested in and listen to what that person has to say.

Step 2: Be clear on what you're asking for. Do you want to come to their office and have a meeting, or were you hoping they'd make time for a quick phone call? Are you asking for a part-time job or an internship? Did you want to meet next time they're in town—at a conference, a speaking engagement, or a stop on their book tour (the way I met Alexis)? A prospective mentor might be less inclined to help you if he or she can't figure out what it is that you want.

Step 3: Back up your request with an example of your work. Sure, you can explain your vision in painstaking detail, but you still need to prove that your work (or passion/goal/project) is as good as it sounds. (Think about it: without some kind of verification, without having *any* examples of your work to share, you'd essentially be presenting yourself as an anonymous sender, and that'd be no good.) A link to your website will put the finishing touch on your fabulous email. Don't have a website? No worries, a simple social media account for your business/ knitting circle/book club can work just as well. YouTube videos count, too.

Step 4: Be polite. There are a lot of people out there— me included—who still believe the most important words in the English language are "please" and "thank you." Hey, it may be corny, but it's true. Being polite is the icing on your mentor-inquiry cake. And who wants to eat a cake without icing?

Step 5: Perfect the subject line. Don't mess up your beautifully worded mentor request with a vague subject line like "Hi." Not only is this totally misleading (your subject line should be crystal clear without being overly long), it's likely that your email will be deprioritized or ignored completely. Consider this: When I receive an email with a subject line like "[Company name] with speaking inquiry," I'm more likely to open that email sooner rather than later, since business inquiries often come with deadlines attached. An email that sounds friendly or social, however, is best to read when I'm hanging out at home on the weekend. Go with something concise and direct, and you'll be less likely to be routed to the spam or trash folder.

Step 6: Don't freak out. Lots of people in the business world receive hundreds and hundreds of emails a day, so don't worry too much if your potential mentor doesn't respond to your inquiry right away. (Remember that everyone's got a life outside the office, too!) There's nothing wrong with sending a second email a week or two after your first, provided you don't become annoying or spammy about it. If you still haven't heard anything after that, don't take it personal. Take a breath and message the next potential mentor on your list.

DETOURS, DERAILMENTS, AND CURVEBALLS

Avoiding Common Traps on the Creative Path

If you know anything about the animation process, you know it's tedious as heck. You have to draw each and every frame (well, you do if you're sticking with traditional 2-D animation), then you have to properly sequence those frames, and if you're drawing by hand, it can be incredibly difficult to correct your mistakes. (If you draw an errant line or something weird-looking on a digital tablet, you can just press a key combination to undo the error; if you're drawing by hand, your only real option is to bust out the Wite-Out.)

At some point in the creative process, then, it's not uncommon for me to get frustrated. I've begun some projects with a whoo-hoo-I'm-gonna-do-a-great-job mentality, only to slide into an ugh-I-gotta-finish-this kind of feeling. I've gotten bored drawing the same background for a particular cartoon over and over. I've worried that a certain character's mouth didn't seem to be moving right. Rarely does my finished drawing resemble the image I had in my head. In fact, when I have a freak moment where the thing I saw in my mind's eye actually makes its way to the screen, I bust out in full celebration.

The thing is, everyone is bound to feel this way at some point or another on his or her creative journey. All creative people experience occasional "artist's block." All of us have moments where the goal we're after—writing an essay, painting a picture, performing a dance move, mastering that athletic maneuver—just doesn't seem possible. Suddenly, we don't have the drive, or we feel discouraged. An unexpected lack of resources threatens to derail our project, or a new deadline throws our whole schedule out of whack. One of the hardest things about living a creative life is maintaining your focus in a world that's full of distractions.

It's also true that in the midst of pursuing that Big Idea, you can lose sight of your original vision. You go in with the intention of X but your project morphs into Y. For example, let's say you start selling your handcrafted jewelry with the intention of sharing your work with the world. Then you make your first sale and everything changes. Suddenly, you start cranking out earrings and cuff bracelets, not because you want to or because you enjoy it, but because you need more things to sell. You become obsessed with the money, or you continue on for no other reason than the feeling that you *have* to.

Or, maybe you're making a short film when, right in the middle of the shooting schedule, your friend suggests a major change to the script. "But it'll look so much cooler if you do it this way," he says. (Cooler to him, at least.) You wind up taking that friend's advice, and by the time you begin the editing process, you cringe: the final product looks nothing like what you intended. *I wish I would have stuck with my original idea*, you think glumly. *I wish I would have been true to my vision.*

There are so many reasons why you might lose focus or veer off course. Even when you think you've got it all figured out, life can still throw you a curveball, a pitch that leaves you swinging wildly when you were aiming for the fences. There's no guarantee that your path will be a straight one, either. (Your Big Idea may evolve and grow and change as you continue to work.) But no matter what detours or derailments you're faced with, there is some good news: you can always get back on track.

Combating Jealousy

So, the only time I really turn green with envy is when someone else in the house polishes off the caramel ice cream—otherwise, I usually just concentrate on doing my own thing. Jealousy, however, is a super-common derailment for creative and artistic people. There's just not much worse than looking over your shoulder at someone who's doing similar work, and believing that he or she is doing it better, cheaper, or smarter than you. Maybe you and someone at your school, for example, are both budding YouTube stars. Well, *she* is anyway: she's getting tons of attention and racking up thousands of views. *Why not me?* you ask yourself at night, in the loneliness of your cold, dark room.

There are two important things to keep in mind whenever you're feeling jealous, bitter, or just plain defeated by someone else's success. The first is that success is not a zero-sum game. What I mean by that is someone else doing well does not prevent *you* from doing well. Someone else's good fortune or hard work or accomplishment does not take anything away from you and your success. Honestly, the world is a big place. There's plenty of room for us all to achieve great things. The second is that maybe (just maybe) you can learn something valuable from this other person. What is it that seems to be working so well for her? Are there any strategies or ideas from her work that you could apply to your own? For example, maybe your "nemesis" isn't necessarily making better or funnier or more informative videos; rather, maybe she's posting them to lots of different video-sharing sites, thereby increasing her exposure as well as her total number of views. Maybe her metadata are more effective (those are the descriptive search terms embedded in an Internet file that make your video or article or blog post come up in someone's Google search). Perhaps you want to reach out to this person and ask her for some friendly advice.

Keep in mind that not everyone is going to want to share his or her hard-won insight and information. That's fine. Forget about those people. Others will be more than happy to share some of their success with you. They might even reveal some of their frustrations and failures, which you can also learn from. (Trust me when I tell you, these people are golden.) Here's something else to keep in mind: it's possible that the very person you're jealous of actually admires the work that you're doing. He might even want to hear more about your experiences. He could potentially become a mentor, as well as a friend. So don't wallow in negative feelings when someone is doing work that seems better or more successful than yours. And for goodness' sake, don't let jealousy deter you from trying something new.

Overcoming Your Fear

One of the best pieces of advice I've ever received came from my mom, moments before I took the stage for my first-ever speaking engagement.

I'd received an email a few days before from a woman named Channtee Gamble, who teaches financial literacy and entrepreneurship to kids at an after-school program in the metro Atlanta area. Turns out, she wanted me to speak to her class. (I'd received some press attention by then, and I was local, as well as, you know, a *kid*, so I guess it seemed like a natural fit.) Of course, I was excited and honored to receive the invitation, but I was more than a little nervous, too. I'd never done any kind of formal public speaking before. I was stepping into the unknown. That can be scary for anyone.

Over the course of the next few days, I wrote and practiced my speech, put together an outfit I'd be comfortable wearing onstage, and selected some designs and drawings to share with the students, all while trying to ignore my growing nervousness. And on the day of the speech, when I climbed into the car to go to the event . . . well, do you ever feel so stressed that you're actually sort of calm? That's basically how I felt the whole ride there.

Later, as I stood waiting for Ms. Gamble to introduce me, I felt my heart lurch whenever I thought about taking those first few steps onto the stage. That's when my mom, no doubt sensing my fear, leaned over to tell me that I was going to do great. And then she said these three magic words: *Do it afraid*. (You'll probably remember that they're the same words she whispered to me before I gave my TEDWomen talk—because it doesn't matter how often you speak in public, it's always nerve-racking.)

Everyone gets scared sometimes, even though whenever we watch someone do something big or brave or seemingly fearless, it's easy to forget that fact. Think about the Olympic diver performing backflip after backflip off that breathtakingly high platform, or the singer who performs on the floor of an arena in front of thousands and thousands of screaming fans. Sure, from where you sit, it may seem like those people just radiate confidence. But for all you know, their hearts were beating a million miles an hour as they waited in the wings, preparing to take that great big stage. In fact, odds are they were incredibly afraid, especially before attempting that *first* dive or singing that *first* song. Absolutely everyone experiences this feeling.

The thing is, fear doesn't necessarily have to be a negative emotion. In fact, when it's channeled properly, it can actually help propel our Big Ideas forward. True, when we're scared of something, it's human nature to start looking for an option that's less scary. It's natural to stop and think, *Now, how can I get myself out of this?* And while the best option may indeed be the scariest, sometimes there are solutions that are better, more efficient, and less stressful. Fear can encourage us to stop and consider our options, to rethink, revise, and perfect our plan. Fear can also encourage us to make new connections, expand our support network, and meet new people. That's because when we're scared of an unknown outcome, we may be more likely to reach out to those around us (as well as to people we don't know, like potential mentors and experts) to ask for advice.

The problem comes when we attempt to ignore our fear, or, worse, when we try to get over it. Fear is a natural, biological response; it can't be suppressed with the snap of your fingers. You can't just will it away. You can't just suddenly stop your fear in its tracks. Yet think of how often people might say to you, in the face of something new or scary or intimidating, "Don't be scared," or the equally unhelpful, "There's nothing to be afraid of." When we find that we *can't* get over our fear, then it's easy to get discouraged or to feel like we've failed.

That's why what my mother told me, as I nervously waited to give my first-ever speech, was so important and transformative. What she was saying is that it's best to acknowledge the fear you feel, and then go ahead and do that scary thing anyway. Rather than try to suppress your fear, it's better to just do it afraid.

With her gentle boost of encouragement, I was able to step in front of the middle schoolers in Ms. Gamble's after-school program and tell my story. I showed them some of the items for sale in my shop, and gave them some advice on how they might start their own businesses. When it was all over, I exited to their enthusiastic applause. Sure, I'd been crazy nervous, but I'd still managed to pull the speech off.

Now, here's the alternative to doing it afraid: not doing anything at all. Fear, if you let it take over, can freeze your creative impulses. It can make you resistant to trying that new thing or searching for that new solution. It can impede the progress you make on your creative path. The scariest thing about fear—when you really stop to think about it—is that it can end up holding you back.

DEEP-FREEZERS AND SPRINTERS: WHICH ONE ARE YOU?

It seems to me that there are two types of people in the world: those who react to fear by shutting down, becoming paralyzed, or freezing in the face of it, and those who respond to fear by barreling forward full-speed ahead, often with little to no concern for the consequences. Figure out which one you are, and you'll reduce the likelihood that fear will derail you and your creative plans.

The Deep-Freezer

Every now and then, we all feel sort of stuck: reluctant to make a certain decision or hesitant to start work on a particular project. You may say to yourself, *I should really finish this* other *project first*, or *I should work on this* other *thing for a while*. That is, you may start making excuses for why you're not moving forward. But are those excuses valid, or are they coming from a place of fear? Are you really just lying to yourself?

It's normal to feel frozen or stuck when you're scared. In fact, being a Deep-Freezer isn't necessarily a bad thing. Pausing for a short time (what I like to call a "minifreeze") can give you a chance to revisit your plan.

With a little time and consideration, you might actually discover a better, smarter path forward.

And while you're taking that pause, it can also be helpful to try to pinpoint exactly where that fear—and the resulting deep freeze—is coming from. Perhaps past experience has made you afraid of failing (you tried it before and it didn't work). Or, maybe you've been discouraged by other people's stories: "Don't do it. I tried it and it was a disaster!" It's also possible—maybe even probable—that what you're feeling is what's at the root of all fear: a fear of the unknown.

Regardless of the reasons why you're afraid, remind yourself: fear is totally normal, and you're not a failure if you can't just get over it. Take a deep breath, resolve to do it afraid (whatever "it" may be), and unfreeze.

The Sprinter

If the Deep-Freezer, well, *freezes* in the face of fear, the Sprinter does the total opposite. She tries to outrun her fear by acting rashly, often without enough planning, research, or time for thinking things through.

Let's try an analogy: Say you and your friend both head to the nursery. You each buy a terra-cotta flowerpot with a mystery plant buried inside. You take your pot home. You water it diligently. You make sure it's getting enough sunlight. And then one day, a tiny sprout pops up from beneath the soil. Sure, it's not much more than a tiny, little green leaf, but you're so excited by this development that you enroll your bud in a flower show. Disappointingly (but perhaps not surprisingly), you lose. Meanwhile, your friend continues watering and feeding her plant, until it eventually explodes into a beautiful blossom. When *she* enters the flower show (months after your failure), she wins

Why did your friend succeed but you failed? Simple: because she didn't rush her flower. You don't want to rush your Big Idea, either.

Every now and then I'll (temporarily) set a project aside when I realize that my idea needs to be fleshed out a little more before it makes sense to get started. If you find that happens to you often—if your ideas frequently fall apart before you can get them off the ground—it may be a sign that you're running too fast. Speeding through life can be just as destructive as restricting your creativity by never taking risks. Some ideas take time to blossom.

Have Faith

What about when things feel totally overwhelming, when you'd rather hide under your bedsheets than come out and face your problems? Well, that's the point at which many of us, myself included, may try to turn to a higher power, something outside themselves. For me, that's my faith.

Everyone has his or her own interpretation of what faith means. Me, I consider God to be like that one best friend who always has more sense than I do. Of course, the general assumption is that he's some big dude who's hanging out in some sort of celestial plane somewhere in the universe (that's Maya-speak for heaven), away from all the ridonkculousness of Earth as we know it, but I think the closer you consider him to be with you, the closer he actually is. I believe that he always has time to come down from his celestial plane somewhere in the universe and hang out for a little bit. He's always there to listen if you just call on him, and he's there to help you through any situation you may be facing, which is what any best friend would do.

Those times when I feel really alone and uninspired, when I'm unsure what to do next? I try to listen to myself and my faith, rather than impose the answer that I think is right (or that should be right) onto a situation. Maybe if I'm having a bad day or something has gone wrong, and I might be wondering, *God, where are you?* I realize that I have to really seek him out and talk to him and reel myself back in from all of those negative emotions and take quiet time to make a connection with him again. It works for me. Maybe something different will work for you.

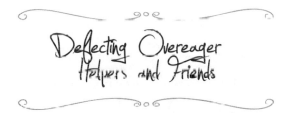

Deflecting Overeager Helpers and Friends

Once your great ideas start to percolate, and once other people begin to see what you're up to, you're probably going to receive a lot of (unsolicited) opinions about the work you're producing. Those ideas can be truly, amazingly helpful. They almost always come from a well-meaning place. And, sure, it's generally a good idea to listen to the members of your support network. They only want to help you succeed, right? Especially when they're telling you how great your idea is . . . except for this *one tiny thing*.

Part of being a creator is having the courage of your own convictions. And as much as you probably love and admire and respect your friends, family, and mentors, it *is* possible to give their ideas too much credence. For example, maybe your friend has a wonderful suggestion, but it would change the core of your idea so fundamentally that it wouldn't feel like *yours* anymore. That's no good.

Being true to your creative ideas means that you'll occasionally have to say no to people—even to close family and friends—in order to do things your way. This is never easy, but it's imperative for you to speak up. Your support network is there to support your vision, not to create its own vision for you. Even those closest to you can (accidentally and unintentionally) undermine your work.

Let's Talk about Haters

A year or so ago, I was perusing the online comments below an article that had been written about me in the paper. Most of them were really supportive and sweet, but one person unleashed a little ball of white-hot hate. She (or he—I have no idea who this person is) said there was no way I'd accomplished any of the things mentioned in the article, that it was much more likely that *my parents* were the ones behind my business.

Now, I didn't bother replying to that person, since that would have been a complete and total waste of my time. And yet I was still irritated. This person didn't know my whole story. He or she didn't know how I got started or where my passions came from. The commenter didn't even know who I really was. So for that person to immediately think, *Oh, she didn't do any of that, because she's only such-and-such age*, well, I'll be honest, it really, really hurt my feelings. I mean, what could be the motive for such negativity? It's not like I'm tossing abandoned kittens into active volcanoes—I run an eco-friendly clothing business.

It's incredibly frustrating when you try to do or say something uplifting and positive and immediately get ridiculed and shot down. Perhaps, though it sounds cliched to say so, this kind of hatred comes from jealousy. (You might have something haters consider "better," and they take out their frustrations about that by blasting you.) Perhaps they feel threatened by you, for any number of ridiculous reasons. (Maybe they're worried that your success will overshadow them, so they unleash a ninja attack of hatred to weaken you.) In rare cases, people may just not be well educated about the work that you do and therefore not fully understand it. And, unfortunately, some people just spread hate for the lulz.

Truthfully, you may never understand what drives someone out there to put down you and your work. But one thing's for certain: negative comments can seriously derail your forward progress. That's probably why my friend-tor Alexis Ohanian says, "Eat your haters for breakfast, like waffles." I'd like to co-sign that.

HATERS, HATERS, GO AWAY

You want to know the easiest way to overcome your haters? The secret to maximum hate deflection? Okay, get ready. This is really big. Seriously, this is some top-secret, high-level information. The secret is . . . *to ignore them.*

I know, I know. I can practically hear your confused and disappointed groans from here. The old just-ignore-them routine isn't exactly new advice, and I know that diffusing negativity isn't always as easy as that. Humans, after all, aren't heartless robots. Whether we like it or not, all of us are emotionally affected by hurtful, inflammatory remarks. Fortunately, I've got ten helpful tips to help you strengthen your hater shield:

1. Realize that haters want your attention. People make mean and negative comments to get a rise out of their target; realizing this is half the battle. It's a little clichéd, but it's still true: ignoring your detractors is a surefire way to drain them of their hater power. Ignore them, and watch as they vaporize into wisps of grumpiness.

2. If you've got a Block button, use it. Most social media websites feature a Block or Ignore button to keep certain people from commenting, reposting, liking, or tagging your stuff; you can often prevent them from viewing your profile altogether. No need for witty comebacks or snarky private messages before you block these folks, either. With a single mouse click, you can send those haters on their hateful way.

3. Don't let one rude comment drown out the voices of those who support you. Have you ever noticed that negative comments seem to affect you more than positive ones? A long, thoughtful message about how much someone loves your work can seem like nothing in the face of one short, ugly comment. Remind yourself: the negative remarks are not more important than the positive ones. Besides, I'd be willing to bet that over the course of six months, you've had ten times more good feedback than bad. When negative comments echo in your brain, try to remember some of the encouraging, helpful, and positive reactions you've heard.

4. Haters deal in opinion, not fact. Just because someone says your art sucks doesn't mean it actually does.

Some persistent haters might even try to "prove" how untalented you are by listing a series of "reasons" why your project or talent or Big Idea isn't great. Those aren't facts, either. Haters don't have the final say on what is and is not valuable or good.

5. It's their problem. If someone dislikes the work you're doing, it's their problem, not yours. It'll only become a problem for you if you choose to make it one.

6. You're not the only one with haters. When you receive a negative or nasty comment, don't bother taking a "Why me?" attitude. You're not some rare case of hater disease. Just about everyone will be affected at some time in his or her life.

7. It's okay to stand up for yourself. Let's say you own a company. Now imagine that the company is a castle, and that warriors from the Kingdom of Hatred have been sent to ambush you for some dumb reason. Whatever you do, *don't* send all your warriors out for a counterattack. Why? Because there's a difference between attacking your haters and defending yourself against them. Just because someone said something unkind does not mean that you need to repeat the behavior. In cases where ignoring your hater isn't an option, you can calmly go about defending or explaining yourself—that's generally the classy way to go. And if you can't think of anything classy to say, just leave them with a smiley face. (It's kind of like saying "screw you" in the most pleasant way possible.)

8. Don't let haters change your mind. Just because someone out there disagrees with what you're doing or who you are doesn't mean that you have to change. Always stay true to yourself.

9. Okay, I don't actually have a number nine, I just wanted this to be an even-numbered list . . .

10. And, finally, DON'T BE A HATER. If someone isn't directly harming you or anyone else, just leave them be. There are already enough lemon chewers in the world, thank you.

Toppling the Twin Terrors: Perfectionism and Procrastination

If you're a perfectionist like me, you want your ideas to be, well, *perfect* before you send them out into the world (a place where people will immediately proceed to judge them, critique them, and rip them to shreds, thankyouverymuch). I used to rework, rethink, and redo my projects constantly, but I couldn't help it: I always wanted to put my best foot forward. Then I heard this wonderful quote that really stuck with me: *Perfection is the enemy of good.*

Here's what that means to me: If you spend all your time trying to make something perfect (which is—let's be honest—nearly impossible), you miss out on a chance to make something useful or good. Perfectionism can quickly and easily morph into a stall tactic. You can easily become so afraid to pursue that Big Idea because you're not convinced you can do it exactly, perfectly right, that you end up not doing it at all. Or, you end up stalling so long that you have to rush to get the thing completed. You put it off and put it off and put it off until—all of a sudden—it needs to be done RIGHT THIS MINUTE. The results can range from tolerable (some people manage to work well under pressure) to downright disastrous (you don't leave yourself enough time to do the work properly). This is why some people believe that perfectionism and procrastination are closely linked. So forget perfect, and settle for good.

IS YOUR IDEA READY TO FLY?

Okay. You've created your Big Idea Strategy. You're got your support network in place. And you're working on avoiding potential derailments. (Sayonara, haters. Adios, fear.) But how do you know that you're really ready to unleash your idea on the public? This is the final checklist I use to determine if my ideas are ready to be pushed out into the world.

✳ What Kind of Feedback Have You Received?

At this point, you've probably run your idea by one or both of your parents, as well as a mentor or a trusted friend. If you haven't, now's the time. What kind of comments are you getting? Are the members of your support network enthusiastic or hesitant? Do they seem excited or more suspicious and concerned? The reactions you get from your inner circle should be a good indicator of the reactions you'll get from a larger crowd. Just remember to give any comments you receive their appropriate weight. What I mean is that there's a clear difference between "That headband is ugly" (which is completely not helpful) and *constructive* criticism ("I think your headbands could benefit from a stronger, more durable fabric"). Asking your support network for feedback isn't about pleasing people, it's about honing your skills. And no matter how enthusiastic or insistent someone may be, you don't *have* to take his or her advice. Trust your gut on this.

✳ Is Now the Right Time?

Sometimes you may come up with a really amazing idea, but now just isn't the right time to pursue it. And that's okay, provided you don't use that as an excuse to avoid pursuing your passions indefinitely. If you think, *I don't have the resources to launch this project right now*, the next step on your creative journey should be figuring out how to get those resources. (Whereas a troublesome or disconcerting response would be, "This idea is too crazy or ambitious, I'll probably never get the resources I need in place.

So why bother?") Taking the time to question and reconsider your options not only helps you grow, it also hones your decision-making skills. It's okay to move at your own pace, so long as you don't hold yourself back.

✳ Are You Having Persistent, Lingering Doubts?

If you're having persistent, lingering doubts, try to determine why. Are those doubts internal (you're worried about looking like a failure) or external (someone else is making you doubt the awesomeness of your Big Idea)? Are you scared of the unknown, or struggling with a tendency to be a perfectionist? Are you feeling jealous of someone else's idea, worried that yours won't be as good? Can you even pinpoint why exactly you feel doubtful?

It's up to you to decide whether or not feelings like these are appropriate or necessary. If all they're doing is getting in your way, go ahead and push forward with your passion. I know that's easier said than done, but it's sometimes good to set your intention ahead of your emotion. And if you need a hit of confidence or inspiration, go back and take a look at your dream board.

You Got This!

People often ask me how I "did it," how I managed to pursue and follow my dreams. The short answer is that I trusted my gut and followed my passion. I believe that creativity always puts you on a path and leads the way forward, revealing your place in the world. The long answer is a little more complicated.

As we go through life, we all travel on different paths at different paces. You might get lost on your trip at times—you might wander down a side road, get stuck in a detour, or even hit a dead end. You might sputter out and feel like you can't move forward. But if you take the time to craft that Big Idea Strategy, build a support network, and commit to your path, you *will* get moving again. It doesn't matter if your Big Idea is to start a business, write a novel, or just to enter your art in an art show, don't be afraid to go forward and share your ideas with the world.

PART THREE

Change Your World

Back when I was seven or eight, not long after my parents and I moved to the house we live in now, I decided that I wanted to start an organic garden. The finished product was nothing too fancy—it's not much more than a small plot in our backyard, a patch of soil sectioned off with two-by-fours (kind of reminds me of a sandbox, actually)—but I was able to grow a veritable bumper crop of fruits and veggies: broccoli and kale, purple carrots (which I didn't even know existed until I found the seeds in the store), blueberries, strawberries, oregano, squash, basil, even watermelon. We also planted a pear tree that produces fruit every year, too.

I don't know if a lot of young people are into organic gardening or if I was just one of a lucky (or perhaps unusual) few. What I *do* know is that I probably had a bit more eco-awareness than your average seven-year-old.

When my dad was my age, for example, he was really into competing in science fairs—he actually won awards from NASA and the US Air Force for his solar energy projects. (I told you he was a pretty tech-savvy guy.) Meanwhile, my mom has always chosen natural and sustainable fibers, nontoxic cleaning supplies, and organic foods whenever possible. I was taught the importance of recycling at a very young age. And I was raised to have love and respect for all God's creatures. (When I was little, I briefly ran a restaurant for the woodland animals that lived in the trees beyond our yard. Specialties included acorns wrapped in lemongrass and berry-and-leaf salad, and I no doubt made a mud pie or two.) So you see, being environmentally conscious isn't just important to me, it's a part of my identity, one of the things that makes me, well, *me*. Which is why I decided, only a matter of days after launching Maya's Ideas, to turn my budding business into an eco-friendly company.

Luckily, I already had some experience with eco-friendly fashion.

For one thing, I've worn vintage and recycled clothing for as long as I can remember. That's because, aside from being less harmful to the environment (the chemical dyes used in some clothing—even the process of *making* the clothes—can pollute the water and air, as well as generate huge amounts of toxic waste), vintage and recycled clothes have character. They tell a story. I mean, I think of myself as a kind of storyteller, whether that's through the act of writing a book, creating an animation, or designing an item for my store (kind of like the story behind Marguerite's Garden, the piece I made in honor of my grandmother). So it just makes sense that I'd want to wear—and make—clothes that tell a story, too.

As I continued growing my business, I started seeking out more and more eco-friendly fabrics to work with, like hemp, burlap, organic cotton, and vintage silks. I experimented with using natural fruit and vegetable dyes and herbal teas when coloring scarves and T-shirts. And rather than feel stifled or hemmed in by the need to make everything eco-friendly, I let my imagination guide me. For example, my mom and I love watching old black-and-white movies, especially those from the 1920s, '30s, and '40s, and that inspired me to make a whole line of cloche hats with vintage beaded and lace embellishments. (When you think cloche, think Angelina Jolie in *The Changeling* or the great dancer-singer-actress Josephine Baker.)

It wasn't just eco-friendly clothes that I sold through my company, either. I also went back to the garden. Since most of the women in my family (especially my grand-mothers on both sides) have a history of making their own scrubs, tonics, and lotions with natural and organic ingre-dients—the deep conditioner–hot oil treatment I use on my hair, for example, comes from a recipe my grand-mother invented and handed down—I've been able to branch out into beauty products. I've got just about every-thing I need to make (and sell!) my hair elixir—organic oils and a blend of herbs—growing in my own backyard.

And these days, my concern for the health of our planet doesn't just figure into my creative endeavors and personal choices (about what to wear, eat, or buy), but into *every* business decision I make. Even my business cards are made from 100 percent recycled, chlorine-free paper.

The necessity of being a good steward to the environ-ment, however, wasn't the only awareness with which I was raised. My parents also instilled in me the importance of giving back. We'd often stock up on canned foods to donate to local food banks. All of our old clothing went to Goodwill or the Salvation Army. And we regularly gave money to local nonprofit organizations or homeless shelters. This was such a natural part of my upbringing, in fact, that I knew whenever *I* started a business, I'd immediately begin to donate some of my proceeds.

Of course, in the beginning, I didn't have much to offer—I told you those first orders trickled into my Etsy store pretty slowly. But whenever I could afford to give, I would. Sometimes that was just ten or twenty dollars, certainly not enough to erase world hunger or to clothe everyone in need. The thing about giving back, though, is that it doesn't matter how small the gift is, it still matters.

Once my business started to take off, I was able to increase the size of those occasional donations to as much as $100 or $200. And within a few years, after I'd gotten some press coverage and national media attention—after Maya's Ideas had exploded into something larger than I could have dreamed—I was able to make a much bigger pledge: a fixed percentage of my profits (rather than a random dollar amount) would go to organizations that I worked closely with and was passionate about. Every year for the last five years, I've given between 10 and 20 percent of my proceeds to groups like the Atlanta Community Food Bank, Hosea Feed the Hungry, the Captain

Planet Foundation, Live Thrive, and the Ian Somerhalder Foundation (an eco-friendly organization founded by the talented actor and humanitarian—I'm a member of their kids' division).

As proud as I was to offer a percentage of my profits to charities and nonprofits, though, I quickly realized that I wanted to do more. I wasn't content to just give money. I wanted to start whole projects that I could shepherd through from start to finish. I wanted to launch my own initiatives that might effect real and meaningful change. I had so many ideas, in fact—after all, I am still a Flip-Flopper—that I realized I needed a way to organize them. The things I wanted to do extended beyond the realm of a clothing line. Which is when I got another one of those Big Ideas: I was going to start my own nonprofit.

I might have been hesitant to tackle such a large undertaking had I not already launched my for-profit business, but starting Maya's Ideas had given me confidence, as well as a sort of blueprint to follow. Just like I'd researched other Etsy shops for help pricing my items, I knew I'd need to research other nonprofits to learn more about how they're organized and structured. Once I'd armed myself with information—step one in that Big Idea

Strategy—I realized that I'd need to file for 501(c)(3) status (that's what allows charitable organizations to be tax-exempt). Finally, I set up a website and started promoting the nonprofit through social media (one of the many things I'd learned how to do). Within only a matter of months, Maya's Ideas 4 The Planet was born.

A few months before the official launch of my nonprofit, I heard about a local reuse-and-recycle event called Metro Atlanta Kids Recycle Day (which was being organized by another one of my friend-tors, the awesome and wonderful Peggy Whitlow Ratcliffe of Live Thrive). The name pretty much says it all—it was an event meant to encourage kids to bring in their recyclables, learning more about environmentalism in the process—and I was pumped. This was, after all, just the sort of event I wanted to be involved with. In fact, the only problem I could see was that Metro Atlanta Kids Recycle Day was on track to be a somewhat small gathering.

It seemed to me that the bigger the event, the greater the impact; I figured the cause could only be helped by

more kids (and their parents) pledging to come out. So I ran to the computer in my mom's office, downloaded the Metro Atlanta Kids Recycle Day logo, imported it to MS Paint, typed out all the relevant information—who, what, where, when, etc.—and printed out a homemade flyer. (Turns out, I was a bit of a graphics ninja, even as a pre-teen. Although I did have to print the flyers in black and white, since our printer was fresh out of colored ink . . . but no matter.) I grabbed my freshly printed stack of flyers and a roll of tape, loaded those up into my little red wagon, and trekked through the neighborhood, taping flyers to people's mailboxes. It was my first-ever act of "activism," and I was hooked.

So, by the time Maya's Ideas 4 The Planet was up and running, I had a new—and even bigger—project ready.

I had already written and illustrated a children's book called *Lucy and Sammy Save the Environment*, the story of two sheep (yes, Lucy and Sammy are sheep), who team up to save the planet from the evil Pollution Monster. In addition to selling the book, though, I realized that I could donate copies to schools and local libraries, as well as give books away at some of my speaking engagements. I also thought it would be appropriate to print the books on 100

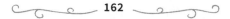

percent recycled paper. Which left me with a new problem: Where was I gonna get the money for that? (Recycled paper isn't cheap!)

Another great thing about giving back is that there's very often an organization or a nonprofit or even a for-profit company out there that can help make your vision a reality. And that's how I discovered the Pollination Project, a nonprofit that provides $1,000 seed grants to social entrepreneurs and change makers around the world. In 2013, I applied for and was awarded a Pay It Forward Loan to print and distribute my book. (Pay It Forward Loans are zero-interest loans; once they're paid back, they're immediately transferred to a new borrower. That means the same $1,000 gets paid forward again and again and again, each time helping a new project and new people.) I was also named to the Pollination Project's Youth Grantmaking Advisory Board, which means I get to weigh in, along with a team of young activists, on who gets the next round of seed grants.

Sticking with the theme of environmental activism, I've since made an animated short starring Lucy and Sammy (when Lucy forgets to pack a blanket for their trip to the beach, she surreptitiously knits one from Sammy's wool, leaving a napping Sammy not only naked, but sunburned!). I have an animated series called *The Pollinators*, about bees and butterflies and hummingbirds that get to be superheroes, in the works, too. I also have BEE A HERO T-shirts (featuring some of the main characters from *The Pollinators*) for sale in my online store. But environmentalism isn't the only thing I'm passionate about, nor is it the only area in which I want to be a force for good, a positive change maker . . .

Sometimes, no matter what social issues you're naturally aligned with, no matter what causes you're naturally passionate about, you hear about a news story or read an article or discover a problem that you're so affected by, you just have to get involved. That's exactly how I felt when I learned that millions and millions of young girls in developing countries around the world miss as many as five days of school a month because they don't have access to—of all things—sanitary pads. What's worse, in the absence of safe and hygienic products to use, these girls turn to dangerous alternatives to deal with their monthly cycles: leaves, rags, cotton, even mud. When you total up all those missed days from school, however, you realize that the problem is much more than a health or hygiene issue, it's a matter of equal rights. When girls miss as much as a quarter of their classes, they fall behind, becoming that much more likely to drop out.

This issue has been in the press a lot lately, and I'd heard that a number of nonprofits had sprung up in recent years in the hope of addressing the global need. That, of course, was excellent news. Of those nonprofits, though, a number of them were donating *disposable* products—and that, to me, seemed a little like trying to put a Band-Aid on a very large problem. (Because what happens when those disposable products are gone?) I didn't want to ignore this issue, or leave it for other people to solve. I wanted to help, too. I just had no idea what to do. How could I possibly affect the lives of girls living in countries like Nepal and Uganda, thousands and thousands of miles from my Atlanta home? Talk about an overwhelming undertaking.

I thought about the issue for months, until one day—wham!—I had another one of those Big Ideas. *I had an eco-friendly clothing company. I had experience* using eco-friendly and biodegradable fabrics. Why couldn't *I* just make some reusable sanitary pads? I immediately started sketching ideas and experimenting, coming up with prototypes and test kits. Sure, I had no idea how to get them halfway around the world. I had no idea if they'd even *work*. But at least it was a small step forward. And if there's anything I've learned, it's that when you get out of your own way, put aside your doubts, and just have faith—when you do it afraid—everything tends to turn out okay. Things have a habit of working out.

Around the time I started making my first prototypes and test kits, I was invited to speak at a MedShare fundraiser. MedShare is a nonprofit that donates surplus medical supplies and equipment from hospitals and medical supply manufacturers to those in need throughout the developing world. It's not just a life-saving health organization (MedShare has donated supplies to nearly one hundred countries), it's also an environmental advocacy group—it has prevented tons (literally *tons*) of perfectly good medical equipment from being dumped into landfills. So, naturally, I was honored to speak at their event. It would also be a great opportunity for me to talk a bit about my sanitary pad project and my desire to help those in need.

I think MedShare and I must have been brought together for a reason, because what happened next can only be described as a sort of cosmic-connection moment: After my speech, the folks at MedShare and I decided to become partners. Medshare, along with a few other organizations I'm working with, is going to distribute the sanitary pads I've been making. As I write this, we're preparing our first shipment for delivery to girls in Nepal, with many more shipments planned. I never could have made a project like this happen entirely alone—my sanitary pad project is yet another example of why a thriving support network is so helpful—but now Maya's Ideas 4 The Planet has a part to play in making a *global* change.

CAN ONE PERSON REALLY CHANGE THE WORLD?

The thing is, I never could have imagined, back when I was eight, making headbands in my studio or asking my mom if I could open an Etsy store, that I'd become a nationally recognized philanthropist, an environmental activist, or a role model. Those were things, in fact, that I never actually set out to be.

Sure, when I first started doing some public speaking, I was sometimes introduced as a role model; I just didn't think much about those words at the time. To me, they seemed like just another title, something to add to the list, like "clothing designer" or "entrepreneur." But once I'd spoken on the TEDWomen stage, once my speech had gone viral and kids and teens from around the world began contacting me to tell me I'd inspired them in some way, that I'd encouraged them to pursue their own passions, that's when it began to sink in.

At first, being a "role model" sounded like an awfully big job. Eventually, however, I realized that most people who are in some way inspirational or influential—including the people whom *I'm* most inspired by—didn't set out to be that way, either. I don't think Rosa Parks refused to give up her seat on that bus because she was trying to become one of the most recognizable leaders of the Civil Rights movement. I don't think the Olympic gold medalist Gabby Douglas became a gymnast because she wanted to motivate young athletes. They each just focused on the thing they were passionate about.

We sometimes think the most inspirational people have to be these hugely famous cultural icons, but that's not necessarily true, either. Very often, people are *most* inspired by those around them, by everyday, ordinary folks. You've probably been inspired by your parents, or your teachers, your pastor, or someone else close to you. In fact, almost everyone in the world is an inspiration to someone, including you. You have most likely already inspired someone out there, whether you realize it or not.

Maybe it's your younger brothers or sisters, or other kids at school (just think how many freshmen idolize members of the senior class, or how much you were impressed by those fifth graders back when you were still in kindergarten). Maybe it's the person you were kind to when others might have bullied or made fun of him.

What I'm saying is, being inspirational doesn't have to be heroic. Changing the world doesn't have to be about making grand gestures. Whatever your contributions, be they as small as preparing someone a meal or as large as launching a charity or sparking a nationwide movement, whether your actions inspire just one person or one million, they have a ripple effect throughout the universe. Even the smallest actions can lead to very big change.

And yet so many of us are too intimidated to even *try* to make a difference. We're too afraid to aspire to something so seemingly monumental as changing the world. Why do you think that is?

Personally, I think there are a few different reasons:

We don't think we *can* make a difference. I believe that most people in the world would absolutely lend a helping hand if they felt like they could. I think that most people genuinely do care about our dwindling natural resources, the pollution of our planet and destruction of wildlife, the hungry and the homeless, human rights issues and violence, animal cruelty and injustice. The problem isn't that people *don't* care. It's that they don't know what to do. The issues plaguing our world can seem so massive that we fool ourselves into thinking they can be solved only with big, bold actions. We're so afraid of not doing enough that, instead, we do nothing at all. We're afraid that we can't make a change, so we don't even try to.

We assume that someone else will do it. Have you ever thought, *There are so many important, better-educated, and more well-connected people out there who are already tackling* [insert important social issue here]. *What do they need my help for?* I'm betting the answer is yes. Now, stop for a minute and consider just how many people out there are thinking this exact same thing. How many people *don't* chip in precisely because they think someone else will? I hope you really think about that. I hope it has a mind-blowing effect. Because the result of that kind of thinking is a whole lot of inaction. It's imperative that everyone do his or her part.

We don't have time to give. This is practically a universal complaint—almost all of us feel stressed, at least some of the time, by the demands of our everyday lives. Work, school, chess club, prayer group, dance class, tennis practice, you name it. But ask yourself: Are you *really* too busy, or is it that you think a particular issue isn't as important as everything else you've got going on, that it isn't worth your time? That may be a sign that your true philanthropic calling lies with a different issue. Go back and study that dream board.

We don't feel like we know enough about an issue to help. You know what? Maybe you don't. Maybe you know virtually nothing about greenhouse gases or the illegal ivory trade or women and girls' rights or worldwide refugee crises. Luckily, a lack of knowledge is an easy problem to solve. You already have lots of practice putting that curiosity of yours to work, don't you?

The first step to getting involved is to overcome this kind of thinking.

It's true that some issues can seem really big or even scary from the outside looking in. Chances are, though, that whatever issue you're thinking of—poverty, breast cancer, environmental injustice, or gun violence—you probably know someone, in your family, your school, or your community, who's been directly affected by it. When you start to realize that something is personal rather than foreign, not only can it motivate you to do something about it, but doing something about it can also seem more manageable, more imperative, and less scary. In fact, tackling something personal is how my friend Mary-Pat got her start.

YOUTH WHO ARE CHANGING THE WORLD: MARY-PAT HECTOR

Antiviolence Activist, Civil Rights Leader, Public Speaker

Age: 17
Hometown: Lithonia, Georgia

At just ten years old, Mary-Pat had already seen the devastating effects of gun violence up close and personal—four of her friends had been tragically killed. Undeterred by her young age, she decided to do something about it.

First, she founded Youth in Action, a nonprofit that tackles issues like bullying, gun violence, and drugs by mobilizing young people to become change makers in their communities. The organization grew quickly, with chapters springing up in multiple states, and Mary-Pat's extraordinary work did not go unnoticed: in 2011, she was given the Woman of Power Award at the twentieth-anniversary convention of the National Action Network (NAN), a civil rights organization founded by Reverend Al Sharpton.

For some people, that might have been enough. But Mary-Pat was just getting started.

In 2013, she joined Usher's New Look, a youth leadership and mentoring organization founded by the Grammy Award–winning singer Usher Raymond, and she learned about the program's Powered by Service grant competition, which awards $500 grants to outstanding public-service initiatives. Casting about for project ideas, Mary-Pat wondered why no one had ever created a shock ad campaign centered on gun violence. After all, shock anti-tobacco campaigns—

which use graphic, gory, or even gross imagery to illustrate the dangers of smoking—had been incredibly successful at lowering teen smoking rates. That's when she got the idea to launch Think Twice, an anti–gun violence campaign that uses graphic images and statistics to encourage teens and young people to "think twice" before picking up a gun. She later received a $50,000 grant from the national nonprofit Peace First, which enabled her to put up forty-five billboards publicizing Think Twice throughout the metro Atlanta area. She also started working with a professional advertising firm to create new Think Twice images.

In 2014, Mary-Pat was named the national youth director for NAN, a position for which she travels an average of four thousand miles a month, speaking at schools, conferences, women's events, and crisis shelters. She also met with President Obama to discuss issues facing today's youth (as well as to receive a Volunteer Service Award). And in 2015, she was voted president of her freshman class at Spelman College. (She ran on a platform of promoting more frank discussions about rape and sexual assault, making her campus more environmentally friendly, and creating a scholarship fund for the future freshman class of 2020.)

At just seventeen, Mary-Pat has already inspired so many people—including me!

MAYA: What inspired you to become an activist?

MARY-PAT: My mom always used to say, "Service is the rent we pay on earth," and that's what I believe. I don't know if I was ever "inspired" to become an activist. I think I've always just enjoyed helping people.

MAYA: What has been the most amazing or exciting part of your journey?

MARY-PAT: Being accepted to Spelman College. I know this is just the beginning!

MAYA: What has been the most challenging part?

MARY-PAT: I would have to say respect. When you talk about civil rights leaders, most people think of older men. In my experience, being a young woman in a national civil rights position means you'll often be challenged and have your leadership skills questioned.

MAYA: What would you say to other aspiring young activists who want to make a difference but don't know what to do or where to start?

MARY-PAT: I'd say just go for it! One of the best things about being young is that you can make mistakes and start over from scratch if you need to. Never be afraid to take leaps of faith. You don't need a college degree or a private school education to validate your worth—the best experience is everyday experience. And finally, be prepared. Learn as much as you can about the topic at hand. It's important to know what you're fighting for.

There are a million issues and movements and organizations out there that could use your help. In fact, there are so many that it can be a little intimidating to try to pick just one or two. If that sounds a bit like how you're feeling, don't be afraid to do a little research first. Sometimes it's just the act of learning about an issue that inspires you to do more, that sparks one of those Big Ideas. Learning about an issue—in his case, environmentalism and eco-living—is what changed my friend Mario's life.

YOUTH WHO ARE CHANGING THE WORLD: MARIO RIDGLEY JR.

Talk Radio Host, Community and Environmental Activist, Public Speaker

Age: 17

Hometown: Palm Coast, Florida

Mario Ridgley Jr. had a mission. The newly elected sixth-grade class president wanted the Imagine School at Town Center, his brand-new charter school in South Florida, to get greener. So he teamed up with Waste Pro of Florida, a professional waste-removal service, to launch his school's first-ever recycling program. The entirely kid-run initiative, called Recycling with a Twist, offered yearly certifications in six different measures of excellence and a Go Green campaign to improve sustainability (not to mention plenty of celebratory pizza parties!). The incentives proved so effective, they have stayed in place for years, long after Mario's graduation.

But that was only the beginning of Mario's journey.

First, Mario was chosen at age eleven to become the first-ever Kid President of Kidstar, a children's educational charity that operates a by-kids, for-kids network of Web-based radio stations. During his tenure, Mario learned all about the fundamentals of radio, which he then used to launch his *own* show. The hour-long weekly program, *Mario Jr. Alive and Green* (which he taped from his home-based studio, with his mom serving as engineer and producer), is all about environmentally responsible living. He's interviewed important environmental experts (like Dr. Rob Moir, the director and founder of the nonprofit Ocean River Institute) and has talked about a wide range of topics, from greenhouse gases to water conservation, from recycling to global warming, always with an emphasis on what kids can do to improve the environment every day. Mario went on to partner with Microsoft in order to broadcast his show live from the Microsoft Store in Orlando, Florida (where kids could come to listen to and participate in the interactive broadcast, learning more about both radio and environmentalism in the process). He also began speaking at local schools, clubs, and businesses, bringing his eco-awareness message to an even wider audience, inspiring people all over the country to live greener lives. How cool is that?

MAYA: What inspired you to become an activist?

MARIO: Let me take you on a little trip down memory lane. Years ago, I was getting ready to compete in my school's first annual science fair. At the time, my parents were in the process of establishing their green consulting company, helping local businesses become more sustainable by shrinking their carbon footprint, so I immediately chose an environmental topic for my science fair project. The official title was "Biodegradable Products vs. Plastic Products," and the idea was to test how quickly each type of product would biodegrade in our earth's soil. Of course, the biodegradable products broke down much, much faster than the plastic products. In fact, the plastic products weren't even affected. After a three-month trial, it looked as though I'd buried the plastic products in soil only the day before. To my joy, I ended up placing first in the science fair. I was pretty excited, as well as overwhelmed, because now I would be headed to regionals, where I would have to describe the project to a panel of judges. But I was actually able to place first again! Now I was ecstatic and feeling quite proud of myself—I really didn't know I would be able to take it this far. The next and final step was going to the state competition, where I placed third (and received an amazing trophy!). I was totally honored by this awesome journey, but I also felt encouraged to do more, to talk to more people about my newfound love for the environment (as well as how putting your best foot forward in school can change your life). I can say that my dad, my mom, and my school are the sole reasons that I became an environmental activist, and I thank them for that.

MAYA: What has been the most amazing or inspiring part of your journey?

MARIO: It's actually *right now*. This is the most exciting and amazing part of my journey, because through you, Maya, I've been given a platform to share that learning is fun and that being smart is cool. I am so grateful.

MAYA: What has been the most challenging part?

MARIO: You know, it really has been a completely fun ride. But one thing I always say is: don't only receive the hard and reject the easy; welcome both for true gratification. Knowledge is a beautiful thing.

MAYA: What would you say to other young activists who want to make a difference but who might be too afraid to get started?

MARIO: Usually, when someone is afraid of something, it's because they don't have enough knowledge about it. So I would tell other aspiring activists to welcome learning. Don't be afraid to research the questions you have about life, or to change the way you think about certain things. Personally, I've changed my life goal at least three different times. When I first started out, I just wanted to be a radio host. Then I thought it would be awesome to have a late-night talk show—I could be like the "go-green Conan O'Brien," talking about the latest and greatest in sustainability. Now I want to go into finance, because I want to help provide funding for other young activists to achieve their visions and dreams. So, don't be afraid to change.

Everyone has a certain thing that they love to do, so go out and do it! There will be trials and tribulations, but don't give up. If you give up, you'll never know if that hurdle you were facing was the last hurdle before seeing your dream become a reality. Believe that you were put on this earth for a reason, and that everything you worked for will come true.

I've been a proud member of the Ian Somerhalder Foundation for years now, after reaching out to Ian and his ISF youth coordinator, Jules Trace. The ISF is an organization Ian started after seeing the devastating effects of the BP oil spill on his own backyard (he's originally from southern Louisiana). The first time I met him, he had a very noticeable positive energy; it was warm and uplifting. What I especially love about his foundation is that it encourages young people, specifically, to do their part to preserve and protect our planet and its creatures. As a member of the ISF Kids/Youth Division, I've written articles and produced videos to promote environmental awareness, focusing on everything from saving the rhinos to learning more about alternative energy sources. We've also got some upcoming projects in the works that I'm really excited about.

Sometimes the way to get started is to reach out to a person or a group that seems interesting, that inspires you. That's exactly what my now-friend Veronica did when she reached out to me and my nonprofit.

YOUTH WHO ARE CHANGING THE WORLD: VERONICA LORYA

Volunteer, Activist

Age: 24

Hometown: Brooklyn, New York

Volunteering her time at school and charity events was just the beginning of a life of service for Veronica Lorya. She has interned at the Erie Housing Authority in Pennsylvania, helping process applications for government-subsidized public housing, and has served as a mentor for students learning English as a second language. While in college at Penn State, she become president of her school's Multi-Cultural Council, an on-campus club that promotes awareness and understanding by working with underrepresented student groups, including the Asian Student Organization, Women Today, and the Association of Black Collegians. These days, she works with AFS Intercultural Programs, a nonprofit organization that offers international exchange programs for thousands of students in more than forty countries around the world. And yet she still finds time to keep doing more: I met Veronica because she wanted to get involved with my sanitary pad project. I'm so grateful that Maya's Ideas 4

The Planet is just one of the organizations to which she's pledged her time, her gifts, and her service.

MAYA: What inspired you to become an activist?

VERONICA: My mother is my biggest influence and inspiration. My family is originally from South Sudan. When war broke out again in the 1980s, my mother and father moved to Kenya to escape the conflict. I was born several years later, only a few months after my older brother passed away from leukemia at the age of fourteen. Then, in 1993, my family suffered another tragic loss when my father passed. He left my mother with the difficult task of raising six children all on her own. I was only a year and a half old.

My mother was determined to provide the life she never had for her children. We moved to the United States, and she worked hard to pay our school fees so that we might one day reap the benefits of success. Her willpower and selflessness instilled in me that I, too, could change a person's life.

MAYA: What has been the most amazing or exciting part of your journey?

VERONICA: The most amazing part is knowing that I'm

making a difference. It warms my heart to know that through my actions I am changing someone's world for the better. That reassurance keeps me going, and excites me for the days ahead.

MAYA: What would you say to other aspiring activists who want to make a difference but don't know what to do or where to start?

VERONICA: My advice for young activists is simple: follow your heart. Use your passion and desire, along with your unique talents, to make a difference in the world. Remember that whether your efforts are big or small, they're still making a difference. Start out small, in your local community, by helping out at food drives, organizing a walk for a specific cause, or volunteering your time to tutor—these are all great ways to give back.

MAYA: Why is it so important for young people, specifically, to get involved?

VERONICA: Because young people are the future. Young people are filled with new ideas and creative solutions when dealing with issues that affect the world. I'm optimistic and determined that, through our collective efforts, we can and will make a difference!

It's also true that you can start your *own* initiative.

I know, sometimes it feels as though your contribution will only amount to a small drop of water in a whole ocean of need. Maybe you have only forty Facebook friends and you actually talk to only three of them anyway—how in the world are you going to start a whole *movement*? But remember that big change starts with small things. Maybe your initiative is a Facebook page about green living, where you list ways that people can get involved with caring for the environment. Maybe you can organize a group of friends and clean up a local park. Maybe it's selling bracelets or T-shirts and giving the proceeds to an organization you want to support. These are some things my friend Taylor did.

YOUTH WHO ARE CHANGING THE WORLD: TAYLOR MOXEY

Chef, Entrepreneur, Philanthropist

Age: 9
Hometown: Miami, Florida

For Taylor Moxey, it all started with a toy.

One Sunday afternoon, back when Taylor was just

six years old, she went shopping with her parents at Target. And as with most every other trip she'd made to the store, she asked her parents for a toy. This time, however, her father said no. Then he gave her a challenge: he told her to come up with a way to earn the money to buy the toy for herself.

Taylor thought about that for a while, until she asked if she might sell cookies and brownies. Her parents agreed to give her a $40 loan for baking supplies—think cookie dough and brownie mix; they even wrote out a business agreement on a napkin—and Taylor got right to work. Then she took her baked goods to church to sell to her fellow congregants after the service. But when she totaled up the money she earned, she realized she had made far more than the cost of the toy she had wanted. Far more than the cost of that $40 loan, too. Taylor had made $175.

That could have been the end of Taylor's story. She could have taken her earnings, bought a whole bunch of toys, and kept right on living her life. Instead, after paying her parents back, she decided to invest in her future. Taylor purchased her very own business cards, which she passed out to teachers, neighbors, and friends. She started making cupcakes from scratch, in addition to her cookies and brownies. She began filling orders from a growing roster of clients and customers. And she decided to enter the KISS Country Midtown Miami Cornbread Competition, an annual event where trained, grown-up chefs compete. Which is when everything changed, because Taylor surprised everyone: *she won.*

Practically overnight, Taylor's budding bakery business exploded. She was featured in a slew of local and national magazines and newspapers, and began taking orders from corporate clients (like Citibank), television personalities (including HGTV star Bobby Berk), and even professional athletes (such as Miami Heat player Joel Anthony). But Taylor still wasn't done, because she knew she wanted to give back.

On a trip to her grandfather's native country, the Bahamas, for example, Taylor was surprised to discover that the residents didn't have access to some of the things you'd find in a big city like Miami—including a library. Taylor decided to open her own library, and to make it eco-friendly and mobile. With help from her parents and some sponsors, she converted an old trailer into a portable learning device. She's also donated a portion of her proceeds to help raise dyslexia awareness (a learning disability that her own father has), as well as sponsored the TECHO organization, a nonprofit that helps build homes for the poor throughout Latin America and the Caribbean.

Who says a nine-year-old can't change the world? I think Taylor is *awesome*.

MAYA: What inspired you to become a baker?

TAYLOR: When I was younger, I would sit and watch cooking TV shows with my mom every day. So when my dad challenged me to come up with a way to make my own money, baking seemed like a natural choice. When I took my cookies and brownies to church, I sold out in just fifteen minutes! And the rest is a piece of cake . . . *literally*.

MAYA: What has been the most amazing or exciting part of your journey?

TAYLOR: The most amazing thing so far has been seeing my Taylor Moxey Mobile Library become a reality. Having complete strangers bring tons of books, toys, and electronics has been amazing. When I was able to help build a home for a family in Haiti by simply selling my cupcakes, it seemed unreal.

MAYA: Why do you think it's important to give back?

TAYLOR: I understand that lots of kids aren't always fortunate enough to have some of the things that I have. But if I'm able to help them and show them how they can start a business, and then use some of that money to help other people, then everyone will be able to chip in!

MAYA: What advice would you give to other young people who want to pursue their passions?

TAYLOR: Try it! It doesn't matter if *other* people don't like your project at first. The most important thing is for *you* to like it, and to not be afraid to mess up.

It doesn't matter how or in what ways you choose to do your part. Your way of giving back might be recycling your paper and plastics or organizing a whole recycling drive at your school or place of worship. It could be donating a few canned goods to a local food bank or volunteering some time each week to serve meals at a homeless shelter. All of these things make a difference, and all of them cause a ripple effect. But now imagine that you recruit just three of your friends to help you. That each of them picks three of their friends, and so on and so forth. Suddenly, it's not just one person giving back—it's a movement. Don't ever let anyone tell you that one person can't change the world.

One person is how every change gets its start.

DISCOVERING YOUR DESTINY

Where Will Your Path Take You?

Before making my television debut on Fox 5 Atlanta, one of our local news shows, I was feeling pretty excited, as well as a little bit terrified. (To quote Pinkie Pie from *My Little Pony: Friendship Is Magic*, another of my favorite childhood cartoons, I was very, well, "nervouscited.") The reporter and her crew had arrived at our house—the bulk of the interview was filmed in my very own living room—so I plopped down into a big red chair, made sure my hair was fixed and that I looked camera ready, stared right into that giant lens, and just started talking. About how I began my journey. About everything I felt passionate about. I didn't have any formal remarks prepared. I just let my passion and positive energy guide me, and the words seemed to just tumble out.

After the main interview, the crew and I headed upstairs to my studio, a.k.a. my creative laboratory. I was eager to show it off, if for no other reason than I'd spent hours cleaning it up the day before—I couldn't have the cameraman tripping over a spool of thread or stepping on a pincushion. (Listen, when you're a creative person, you usually end up creating a messy workspace.) I unveiled some of my designs and played some of my animations, wondering what the final cut would look like, and if the producers would keep any of my favorite parts.

On the day the interview actually aired, my parents and I huddled around the television. I'll admit that it was weird to see myself on TV, especially on a channel I'd been familiar with all my life (there's maybe nothing as recognizable as your hometown network news program), but I was really happy to see how the package had come together—they did, indeed, keep the majority of my favorite parts. After the segment had aired, we were all clapping and cheering, but it was in that moment that I realized Maya's Ideas had become something much bigger than me. I'd been able not only to give back in some ways, but also to make a larger impact than I could have imagined. It was like there was some outside source, or a higher power, guiding me on my journey.

It wouldn't be the only time I felt that way.

Several years later, when I was in San Francisco and preparing—nervously, you'll remember—to give my TED-Women speech, I went backstage to get my hair and makeup done, and there, standing right in the middle of the room, preparing to give *her* talk, was the amazing, incredible Diana Nyad. Now, if you're not familiar with Diana, you need to do some serious research. She is a record-holding, award-winning long-distance swimmer who became the first person to swim the more than one hundred miles from Cuba to Florida (on her fifth attempt, at the age of sixty-four); understandably, her story of determination and perseverance has inspired people all over the world. I, however, was completely shocked to see her. I'd had no idea she was one of the TEDWomen speakers. In fact, I'd only recently watched an episode of Oprah's *Super Soul Sunday* that featured Diana, and I had been captivated by her story. So to go from sitting there in my living room, riveted to the TV, to actually meeting her—much less sharing a stage—was mind-boggling. But what *really* blew me away would happen a year or so later.

I had been organizing my studio when I came across an old article about me from the *Atlanta Journal-Constitution*. It had been published in September, just a few months before I made my TEDWomen debut, and right there on the exact same page as my article, just a little down and to the left, was an article about Diana.

You see, I don't think it was a coincidence. I think she and I were destined to meet.

As I stood there gawking at her, she walked right up to me and introduced herself. The memory is now too much of a blur for me to remember exactly what she said, but the gist of the conversation was that she was curious to know who I was and what I was going to be speaking about—all of us had been making the same sort of small talk. But she seemed particularly interested in my story, and was really supportive of the ways in which I was giving back.

Diana took the TED stage right after me, and in the first few minutes of her talk, she singled me out in the crowd, using me as an example of women and girls in the world doing awesome work. I beamed from my seat in the auditorium. I had made not only a new friend, but a new personal she-ro.

I have had a magical, unexpected, occasionally out-landish life so far—I know I've been fortunate to experience some amazing things—but truthfully, I don't think any of it has sunk in yet, and I'm not sure if it ever will. I don't know where my life will take me, or what's going to happen next, or what the future will bring. None of us do. What I *do* know is that we all have a creative gift to share, a way to influence the world, and the power to make our dreams a reality. I don't believe in coincidences. I think we all have a purpose in this life, a destiny.

What will yours bring?

WHAT NOW?

s you near the final pages of this book—since I'm not able to throw you a party, I wanted to at least include some confetti between the pages, but my publisher wouldn't allow it (it's the thought that counts, right?)—I hope you have more confidence in your creative abilities, and that you're eager to share those gifts with the world. To all my fabulous Flip-Floppers, beautiful Blank-Drawers, and unsurpassed Under-Thinkers, I hope that you're happy being whatever type it is that you are. I hope you know that if you still aren't sure which passions to pursue, that's okay. You are still an artist, a visionary, and an inspiration. I hope you stand firm in your weirdness and strong in your awkwardness. Be proud of your wonky fan art and your failed lines of code. Use your typos and missed kicks on the field as symbols of your power. Take that measly five dollars you made at the lemonade stand and buy yourself something nice. Swing that homemade polymer clay necklace around your neck and wreak some havoc. We're all just awkward little jelly beans making our way through the jar.

But we're creators, too.

So go out and create the world you want to see. And make it *awesome*.

THANK YOUS

GOD, for all of the blessings and guidance

My parents, Deidre and John Penn, for their endless love and support

My great aunt Pauline Avant (Aunt Ba Ba)

My great grandmother Josephine Penn

My grandparents John and Gloria Penn

All my aunts and uncles (especially Janie, Toni, Mickie, and Stephen)

All my cousins (especially Micah, Aaron, Sophia and Phil; love my cuzzos)

My brother John (Thanks for your support, bro.)

My BFF Madisen G. (Thanks for all the weird inside jokes and putting up with my Maya-ness.)

The squad (Thank you for always being there. I love you nerds with all my heart.)

Michele Martin (I loved you from our first conversation. We are truly kindred spirits. Thank you for having the same vision.)

Courtney Hargrave (a.k.a. Angelic Ninja) for all of her hard work

Michelle Howry, Hilary Mau, and my family at North Star Way and Simon & Schuster

My furry babies (Blackberry, Fritter, and Coconut, a.k.a. The Trailmix Trio, and Shelldon)

Maureen Ferrell

Tacoma Perry

James Coney

Audrey Jones

Chef Evelyn Paul

Chris Anderson, Pat Mitchell, Kelly Stoetzel, June Cohen, and my TED family

Ariel Nessel and Alissa Hauser and my TPP family

Ambassador Audrey Gardner

Shelia Poole

Sara Bernard

Kara Ohngren

Kenny Leon and Jennifer Dwyer McEwen

Gabrielle Bernstein (You rock! Thank you for being an inspiration.)

Nikki Reed (Thank you for your beautiful heart and generosity and all that you do.)

Nicki Escudero (Nicki a la Noche) Thank you for your support and friendship!

Jamie Broadnax (Black Girl Nerds)

Dan Carroll (DragonCon)

Jules Trace

Ruth Pittard

Priscilla Woolworth (author of *LOLA Lots of Love Always*)

W. Imara Canady

Daniel Troppy

Krista Hayes and Michael Baisden

Watermarke Church/Woodstock City Church/Northpoint, Andy Stanley, Gavin Adams, my church smallgroup and my smallgroup leader Ms. Leslie

To my customers, supporters, everyone who has sent inspirational and life-changing emails, prayed for me, and prayed over me, thank you, thank you, thank you.

ABOUT THE AUTHOR

Courtesy of Maya Penn

Maya Penn is an award-winning artist, animator, writer, illustrator, philanthropist, environmental activist, filmmaker, eco-designer, entrepreneur, coder, and keynote speaker. She is the CEO of Maya's Ideas, a company she started in 2008 when she was just eight years old. She creates eco-friendly clothing and accessories.

She loves to use her creativity to give back. Ten to twenty percent of her profits go to local and global charities and environmental organizations. She started her own nonprofit called Maya's Ideas 4 The Planet, where she is working on an ongoing project to give back to girls in developing countries. She also helps girls pursue their passions in technology and STEM fields.

She has been featured in Forbes, *Time*, NPR, CNN, *O Magazine, Essence, The View, The Steve Harvey Show, Huffington Post, The NRDC, Entrepreneur Magazine, Wired, Black Enterprise, Cosmopolitan, Ebony, The Atlanta Journal-Constitution*, and many other publications. She's done three TED talks. Maya's TEDWomen talk has gone viral, with more than a million views worldwide. Maya is the youngest female to do two back-to-back official TED talks.